BRIGHT IDEAS

Inspirations for WRITING

Published by Scholastic
Publications Ltd,
Villiers House,
Clarendon Avenue,
Leamington Spa,
Warwickshire CV32 5PR

© 1991 Scholastic Publications Ltd

Written by Sue Ellis and Gill Friel
Edited by Juliet Gladston
Sub-edited by Catherine Baker
Designed by Sue Limb
Series designed by Juanita
Puddifoot
Illustrated by Nick Ward
Cover artwork by Nick Ward

Designed using Aldus Pagemaker
Processed by Pages Bureau,
Leamington Spa
Artwork by Alan Grant, Designer
Printed in Great Britain by
Ebenezer Baylis & Son, Worcester

**British Library Cataloguing in
Publication Data**
Ellis, Sue
  Bright ideas : inspirations for writing.
  1. Primary schools.
  Curriculum. Composition (Arts).
  Teaching
  I. Title II. Friel, Gill
  372.623044

  ISBN 0-590-76561-2

CONTENTS

The authors wish to acknowledge the
following children whose work is
reproduced in this book: Keira Baird,
Amy Blount, Lucy Burns, Steven
Craven, Robert Downing, Barry
Fitsimmons, Benjamin Flight, Anne
Friel, James Friel, Catherine Gray,
Derek Hamilton, Neil Henry, Rhona
Heron, Jodie McGuiness, Kevin
Meechan, Paul Murray, Lynn Norman,
Eleanor Partridge, Stuart Phifer, Jason
Richardson, Laura Smith, Lorna Smith
and Laurence Turner.

INTRODUCTION

Writing

Why is it that many children love listening to stories, telling stories, acting out stories, reading stories ... but hate 'creative writing'? Why do they love doing science activities, talking about science activities, explaining science activities ... but hate writing up a science experiment?

Why is talking to children about writing such an interesting yet salutary experience? Unfailingly, they describe themselves and others in absolute terms; you're either a 'good writer' or a 'bad' one, and the ability to write is seen as a God-given gift which some have and others, quite simply, don't.

The work of teachers and researchers such as Donald Graves and Lucy Calkins has greatly influenced the way writing is taught in schools today. They have clarified the writing process so that teachers have a clear framework within which to work. However, over the last few years the pace of educational research and change in all areas of the curriculum has been tremendous. Teachers are left breathless after working out the many practical implications of the new, exciting ideas they want to include in their teaching. Any teacher can tell you that time to think, reflect and devise new ways of working is in short supply. Teaching is exhilarating, but teachers leave new ideas untried because it is a full-time, demanding job.

BACKGROUND

This book has been written for teachers who love teaching. Good, successful teachers who want to try some new ideas (or even old ideas presented in new ways) but who haven't the time to work them all out from scratch. It translates research ideas into practical, tried and tested teaching activities, explicitly demonstrating how these could be presented and organised with a large class of children.

Successful writers

Before we talk about classroom activities, however, let's think briefly about writing. What is it that makes a good writer? And, just as important for the subject of this book, what makes a good teacher of writing?

It is clear that successful writers believe that the ideas they write down are important. They know why they are writing them and who is likely to read them. They have thought about how best to express their ideas so that the reader will understand, and they know that sometimes they need to try out several different ways in order to decide which is best. They are able to transcribe their ideas quickly and skillfully, recognising when neatness is a priority and when it is not. Often the most successful writers have very firm opinions about *how* they will get their writing read by others.

In short, successful writers are driven by a sense of purpose and a sense of audience. They have the understanding and ability to order and express their ideas effectively in language. They can write quickly and fluently and appreciate the role and importance of good presentation and of publication.

Successful teachers of writing

What, then, has a teacher to do in order to teach writing well? The answer seems at once both simple and all-embracing. In simple terms, a successful teacher provides all the conditions required for

successful writing. She ensures a meaningful context which provides the children with both an audience and the motivation to write. Knowing that it takes time to create such a context, she considers writing opportunities carefully when planning her work. Her lessons are structured in a way that helps the children to express their ideas, sort them out and order them. Discussion sometimes enables the children to do this, but sometimes it entails a hard and solitary struggle demanding concentration and time. To help, she teaches the children word-processing skills and how to draft and redraft their work until both thinking and meaning are clear. She listens to the children and sets high standards. She shows them how to write fluently and legibly, and insists that they practise these skills to build up speed and accuracy. Finally, she recognises how important it is to encourage the children to take a pride in their work and an interest in the work of others, and builds up children's awareness of how to use display and presentation to entice their readers to read on.

Throughout, the successful teacher is sensitive to the children's needs, recognising what is required and providing for it, and eventually teaching the children to articulate their own needs.

If you are beginning to feel a little crumpled beside this paragon of virtue, take heart. She is simply the teacher

inside all of us without the constraints under which we work.

How to use this book

It is hard to present practical ideas on how to teach writing without specifying both what the child will write about and how the urge to write can be inspired. The activities in this book therefore indicate writing tasks for children, and also the contexts in which they could be meaningfully presented.

Setting up meaningful contexts takes both teaching and planning time. Chapters 3, 5 and 7 are devoted to 'Writing in a context' and detail three topics, each aimed at a different age-group ('Ourselves' for infants, 'Holidays' for middle schools and 'School' for upper juniors). Each topic generates a number of writing ideas.

Although we have suggested that the activities within these contexts are appropriate for particular age-groups, many could be easily adapted in order to suit a different age-group or a slightly different topic, or could be used as individual activities.

For those situations where it is not possible or desirable to embark on an extended topic, we provide several chapters of ideas which generate their own contexts and can stand alone.

This book can therefore be used in several different ways. Teachers can dip into it for one-off lessons, or use it as the basis for planning the work of a class.

A teacher could, for example, choose the most appropriate topic context and work right through all the activities suggested, beginning with the tasks set in the collaborative writing chapter. This would give the children an extremely comprehensive experience of writing for possibly one term of the year. Within the topics all aspects of written language may be

explored, and many links with other areas of the curriculum will arise, resulting in an integrated project.

Single chapters make interesting mini-topics, and children needing practice in discrete areas such as functional writing could, with some adaptations, work through one, two or even all the contexts suggested.

The contexts may also be used as exemplars of how to build written language coherently into any chosen topic. Discrete ideas suggested in Chapters 2, 4, 6, 8 and 10 may become starting points for interesting mini-topics, or could be adapted and worked into any topic being studied by the class.

There are obvious opportunities for organising whole-school projects, extending the theme up or down the school as appropriate. Special years in the school calendar, for example Silver or Golden Jubilees, might call for a whole-school project on 'Our school'. 'Holidays' would make an appropriate school theme for the summer term while 'Ourselves' is suitable for use at any time of the year. Work in school that is planned and evaluated by groups of teachers increases collegiality and shared responsibility, so that teaching becomes more dynamic and less stressful.

The 'Schools' theme suggested for upper juniors can make an interesting primary/secondary liaison project for children about to move on to a new school. Many of the activities are also suitable for early secondary classes in that they target particular writing skills.

In Chapter 1, 'Collaborative writing', we have been explicit about how to structure activities, and teachers will be able to copy and adapt these ideas to any curricular area or theme.

Display ideas suggested in the chapter on presentation and display provide ways not only of sharing children's work with new audiences, but of surprising the children and decorating your classroom, or indeed your school, for celebrations and special occasions.

Finally, we strongly recommend that anyone using this book begins by reading Chapter 1 on collaborative writing. This not only gives good starting activities for themes, but contains much practical advice about implementation, knowledge of which is assumed in all the other chapters.

CHAPTER 1

Collaborative writing

Anyone entering a modern primary school will find children working in groups. Teachers group children for a variety of reasons and in a variety of ways. Various forms of ability grouping, topic grouping and social grouping are common. However, this does not mean that the children work collaboratively. It is common to find the children working within these groups as isolated individuals, rarely discussing or sharing their work with each other.

Collaborative group work is different. Here, the child's initial ideas are always further inspired or modified by discussion with others; it is a dynamic process in which children share, challenge and refine their ideas. The final piece of work may be a joint effort or several individual pieces, but the group discussion will have played a central, formative role in the end result.

BACKGROUND

Some of the problems

Teachers worry about this sort of group work in class. One concern is that the children will not participate equally; some will dominate and others acquiesce, 'coasting' the lesson, safe in the knowledge that they will be able to copy the work of a more dominant or conscientious child.

Another worry is that the classroom will automatically become noisy and disorganised – that it will become harder to keep tabs on individual children and to monitor their work and progress.

A further issue concerns the role of the teacher. There is a general, but unfounded, idea that with collaborative work this becomes less central. This is closely linked to another fallacy; that collaborative work is less structured and that less 'real learning' goes on.

It is true that badly planned, badly taught collaborative work will not result in a good learning experience. But this is true for any teaching. Some teachers believe the myth that if children are left alone, with no specific guidance about how to work, they will collaborate successfully. They won't. If you try to do it this way, you can be sure that it will end in tears (yours, the children's or both).

Successful collaborative group work has to be *more*

structured, and initially this structure must be provided by the teacher, because most primary children have yet to develop the organisational ability or social skills to structure their own work patterns.

Why learn collaboratively?

It is clear that we all make sense of new knowledge and information by integrating it into what we already know. To do this, it is helpful to re-explain the knowledge in our own words and to bounce ideas off others. The teacher who attempts to be the sole sounding-board for the 30 or so individuals in his or her class will either overlook some children or have a nervous breakdown. Collaborative group work is about teaching children how to do this for each other. It is not a case of the brighter children helping the slower ones, but of children working together so that they all increase their understanding.

Why collaborate in the writing process?

It is rare for adults to write alone, without collaborating at some stage. Certainly, the first draft of a letter to the bank manager will be discussed at some length with another adult: 'Try being more obsequious'; 'A few more "sorries" and "pleases" wouldn't go amiss.' Even the note to school for a sick child may be altered after a 'Don't say I've had that. It's embarrassing.' Sensitive school reports will be discussed at length with colleagues, and the final draft of a school curriculum will have resulted from close collaboration with several concerned groups.

This critical discussion and sharing of ideas helps us to organise our writing into a more acceptable finished product. Children who are writers need the same opportunities to test their ideas of writing structures on others. Just as for adult writers, collaboration between children can take many forms and have many different outcomes, sometimes shared, sometimes individual.

We know, both from our own practice and from research, that standards of writing can improve dramatically as a result of collaboration.

Advantages of collaborative work

Collaborative work usually increases a child's involvement, which in turn increases motivation. When the task is suitably structured, children can be given more control over their work – and they find this exciting.

If you have ever felt deflated when, after a good lesson, the children have produced disappointingly similar pieces of writing, collaborative work may provide a remedy. With collaborative work, instead of getting 30 pieces of writing which reflect the children's ideas filtered through a single teacher's response, the different groups provide a variety of origins and routes for inspiration and the development of ideas. Originality and diversity thrive.

The social side is important too. Through collaborative group work, children become more self-aware and more sensitive to others. Knowing how to collaborate effectively with others involves many sophisticated social skills, and without opportunities to practise these essential talking and listening skills, many of our children will grow up unable to operate in this crucial area.

Rules and routines

The atmosphere required for collaborative work is one of trust and respect. Responsibility is given and accepted. The children must work within a system of rules and routines where the boundaries of freedom are known and clearly defined.

Before a class is ready to try collaborative work, some basic rules and routines must be firmly established. In her book *Change: One Step at a Time*, Lois Napier-Anderson describes in a clear, practical way how to establish routines.

The initial routines that she suggests are simple:
• Don't bother anyone.
• Don't interrupt a teaching or discussion activity.
• Put things back after you have finished using them.

• Put your name on your work.
• Put finished work in a regular place and know the routine for storing unfinished work.

She then describes how to add to these, gradually allowing children more freedom while making the boundaries of that freedom clear. Additional routines that are particularly important for collaborative work are:
• Know where to find equipment and how to use it.
• Know what to do if you finish work early or are in difficulty.
• Know, and obey, signals which indicate 'ten minutes left' and 'finish up now'.

If you feel that your current class will never be like this, do not despair. Read on – this book has been written for you.

It is difficult to change behaviour and you must accept that there are no instant solutions. Success will only be achieved step by step, slowly altering the environment and individual expectations, allowing the children time to learn new ways of behaving and of accepting responsibility for their own learning. Begin by establishing the basic routines, introducing new ones only when the old have become automatic.

Initial assessment

Before introducing any work programme which relies heavily on collaborative skills, you need information about the current range of skills in the class. One way of getting this is to set a highly structured collaborative task and observe how the children cope with it. Activities 1 to 3 (pages 15 to 17) can be used for this.

If the children have not done much collaborative work before, you will probably find that during the early stages many make a disastrous first attempt, and then improve in leaps and bounds. For these children it is a question of making them aware of how they should behave during collaborative work, and setting the ground-rules.

Other children have genuine difficulty in listening to their peers, justifying their own opinions, resolving differences, compromising, and all the other talking, listening and social skills which underlie the collaborative process. Initial assessment of the class should concentrate on recognising those children who have genuine difficulty.

Some teachers may feel guilty about doing this. After all, they reason, if they're not actually teaching, are they really earning their money? The answer has to be a resounding 'yes'. The information gained from such observation is essential if future collaborative work is to be successful.

Preparing for the tasks

It is important that the children are in the right frame of mind to do this sort of work – steer clear of sports day, windy days (always guaranteed to make the children excitable), or the last day of term. The time of day chosen should also indicate that you value the work.

Seating arrangements should give the children space to write and draw, yet allow them to talk easily without having to shout across the table.

There are no firm rules about how to organise or choose the working groups. Some teachers prefer to begin with friendship groups and let the children choose their groups. Some assign children randomly to groups by allocating each child a number between, say, one and six, and getting the 'ones' to form a group, the 'twos' to form another, and so on. Others would rather set up pre-arranged groups, choosing children to achieve a mixture of skills, insights, personalities or curricular strengths. Assigning children to pre-arranged groups can introduce a more businesslike attitude, remove the established 'pecking order' in some friendships, and encourage children to think for themselves.

Any new group will require a familiarisation period before the children start working really well together. For this reason, it is suggested that the children work in their pairs or groups for several lessons in succession. You will probably find it useful to make some brief notes after these sessions.

Presenting the tasks

Before presenting a task to the groups, decide how much time you will allocate to each part of the task and be sure to let the children know this, since being able to pace work is an important skill.

Introduce the tasks by telling the children that they are going to try a different sort of activity. Describe what they will be doing and ask them what type of behaviour they think is desirable when doing this sort of work. Some of the things they might mention are:
• listening to each other, and showing this by focusing attention on the speaker and asking questions;
• taking turns to speak, and not shouting each other down;
• sticking to the task and not 'mucking about'.

Before they start, make sure that the children know how you want them to work, and understand that afterwards they will be asked to discuss both the work itself and *how* they worked.

What to look for

Start by considering the groups.
• Look for groups that are slow to make a proper start. Is this because there are particular individuals who will not sit down or listen, or is the cause less obvious, with no single child at fault?
• Look for groups where everyone is talking and nobody listening. It is common for such groups to contain some members who have 'opted out' and appear totally uninterested; note these individuals.
• Look for groups that are working very successfully, giving each other time and space to explain ideas and give reasons for opinions.

Next, look more closely at the behaviour of individuals. Some children may be asking questions, seeking explanations and clarifications, showing an awareness of the need to involve others, keeping others to the point, and justifying their own opinions.

Other children will be less skilled at collaborative work. They may do some or all of the following:
• interrupt;
• shout others down;
• talk a lot but rarely listen (often showing this by having little eye-contact with speakers or by behaviour which distracts attention from the speaker);
• interfere with the work of other groups;
• sidetrack their own group.

Such children can be helped in two main ways; in the first place, by pointing out specific behaviours which are unproductive. Children must be made aware of behaviour that is uncollaborative, and be encouraged to discuss ways of dealing with it. With consistent feedback and good teaching, children will come to recognise these situations before they occur, rather than in retrospect. Second, groups can be taught to work within structures that actively promote the desired behaviour – turn-taking, questioning, explaining and justifying opinions, or any other collaborative skill.

What to do if chaos ensues

First of all, keep your cool. Stop the class and remind them about the atmosphere required for work, the noise level that is acceptable, and so on. Ask if anyone has particular problems with the work, and deal with these. Praise the children who are working well.

Choose some children who are particularly noisy or disruptive and ask them to explain what has happened in their group so far. They will either name individuals who are behaving badly, or one child will say something like 'Everyone keeps shouting out'.

Telling the children not to do this is not sufficient at this stage. Instead, ask each child to think about his or her own behaviour in the past few minutes. What was each trying to do? Did it have the desired effect? Ask what other strategies they might have used, and take suggestions from the whole class; advice from peers is usually respected in such circumstances. Your approach should be one of analysis, not blame.

Remember, however, that this is an interruption to the children's work, and keep it as short as possible – a few minutes at most. The children will learn most by *doing* the collaborative tasks, and must be given time to practise.

The activities

The following tasks can be used as independent activities to introduce collaborative work to a class unused to working in this way, or as a 'way in' to a larger, more sustained piece of work.

We have intentionally structured the activities so that the process of collaboration can be observed, assessed and discussed. If your class will generally find any of these activities too difficult to complete without help, then simplify the tasks; for example, by asking the children to draw rather than write lists.

When a group is working together for the first time, it is important that the task is tightly structured to ensure that only a few decisions need to be made, but that each member participates in the decision-making process. Thus the tasks require the children to make and record individual decisions first, without discussion. These decisions then form a written bank of ideas on which the group discussion and collaborative work can be based.

Initially, it is a good idea to ask the children to collaborate in pairs. This is good advice for the start of any new project and applies even when a class is used to working collaboratively. It allows an opportunity to re-establish the ground rules for working together within the new context.

The larger the decision-making group and the more open or complex the task, the greater the number of possibilities. This obviously leads to a more complicated decision-making process and a greater potential for disagreement.

The limits of collaboration

We have devoted this chapter to a consideration of how collaborative group work might be introduced to a class unused to working in this way, but we do not suggest that the dynamic process of collaborative writing should always replace individual work. Indeed, we believe that there are many times when children need space and silence in order to formulate ideas and develop their own style. It is essential that a balanced programme for teaching writing should also provide this.

ACTIVITIES

1. Introductory activity: the school tuck shop

Age range
Six to eleven.

Group size
Individuals, pairs and the whole class.

What you need
Photocopiable page 162, scissors.

What to do
Tell the class to imagine that they have been put in charge of the school tuck shop. Brainstorm all the things which would be good to sell. This should be done very quickly and with limited discussion. Ideas should be written swiftly on the chalkboard or a large sheet of paper.

Give each child a copy of photocopiable page 162 and ask them to decide the six things they would most like to sell in their tuck shop. Emphasise that this is a personal decision, and because you want *their* opinion, the work must be done without discussion and in secret. They can use ideas from the brainstorm to help them consider all the possibilities, but they must think carefully before making their choices, for they will have to justify them later.

Allow three or four minutes for this part of the activity, and warn the children when they have one minute to go. Check that all the children have recorded their decisions before moving on to the next stage.

Put the children into pairs and tell them to show and explain their decision sheets to their partners. As a pair they must compile one joint list of six items between them. They must both agree on all the items in the final list, which may use ideas from their individual lists, or new ideas which are compromises. Some children may find it easier to sort the decisions if, after explaining them to their partner, they cut them up so that each is on a separate piece of paper.

The pairs must then agree an order of priority for their six items, starting with the most important. Allow up to ten minutes for this part of the activity and warn them when they have five minutes and one minute left.

Once the children have finished the sorting exercise, draw the class together and discuss both the results and the collaboration. Did the children find it easy? Did they enjoy it? Did any of them argue or feel hard-done-by?

Try always to give clear and explicit feedback to individuals about how they worked. You may find that some pairs constructed their list with no discussion at all, simply taking it in turns to make choices. It must be made quite clear that although in one sense this is fair, it is not what is required.

Find out if anyone failed to get *any* of their original decisions on to the final list.

Was this because of an over-dominant partner or because they did not take the opportunities offered? Find out how the pairs started their discussion. Ask the children to comment on how well they feel they and their partners were able to justify their opinions.

Follow this by asking how well children thought their partners listened to them and considered their point of view. Compile a class list of useful questions to ask. This might include the following:
• Which is your best idea, and why?
• Which of your partner's ideas do you like best, and why?

Discuss why such questions are useful. Finally, ask how differences of opinion were resolved, and if you have time, start a list of useful strategies for resolving conflicts.

To stimulate discussion, you may use your own observations of particular pairs working, but make sure that you invite the children concerned to comment on what you saw before using them as examples to make a general teaching point.

The work produced should be made into some sort of display, no matter how temporary, showing individual decisions and the final lists produced by the pairs.

Further activity
As a result of the discussion and your own observations, you may choose to structure the next task in a particular way. For example, if you feel that the children are not really sharing their ideas, build this into the structure of the next activity by giving each child two minutes to present and explain his or her individual work before any discussion

takes place. If you feel that some children are too dominant, make them particularly responsible for asking questions next time.

2. Introductory activity: a space adventure

Age range
Seven to eleven.

Group size
Individuals, pairs and the whole class.

What you need
Photocopiable page 163, writing materials.

What to do
Ask the children to imagine that their space rocket has crash-landed on a strange planet. It is their job to make a preliminary exploration of the planet and report back to Earth. At this stage, they know nothing about the planet and what they might find, except that they will be unable to carry more than six of the things listed on photocopiable page 163 with them on their journey of exploration. They must choose which things to take.

Follow the method for collaborative decision-making suggested in Activity 1 (page 15). Begin with each child making an individual list of things to take, and then ask the children to discuss the lists in pairs and compile a joint one. If you have previously done Activity 1 with the class and you feel that they coped well with working in pairs, you may like to ask them to work in groups of four this time. Once

the joint list has been agreed upon, the children should prioritise it.

As with Activity 1, it is extremely important to follow this activity with a discussion both of the results and of how the children worked together. The format and questions for this discussion will be broadly similar to those outlined in Activity 1 (see page 15). If the children worked in larger groups of three or four, you may like to ask them to comment on whether they felt it was easier or harder working in the larger group.

Further activity
The children can be asked to draw a map of their planet and to write about what happened when they began to explore it.

3. Introductory activity: more collaborative decisions

Age range
Six to twelve.

Group size
Individuals and pairs.

What you need
Photocopiable page 164, rough paper.

What to do
Before you attempt this activity, remind the class of the previous discussions they have had, and tell them that this is another opportunity to practise a collaborative way of working.

Give each of the children a copy of photocopiable page 164 and ask them to complete each section on their own,

under the same conditions as before. The photocopiable sheet asks them:
• If you could grant three wishes for your class, what would they be?
• If you were the headteacher, what four rules would you have in your school?
• Which four famous people would you choose to go on holiday with, and why?

Allow the children a fixed amount of time to complete their answers. When individual decisions have been reached, tell the children to form pairs. Only if the class has successfully done Activities 1 *and* 2 should you consider allowing them to form groups of three or four.

Each pair must decide which of the three topics on the photocopiable sheet they wish to pursue. Having decided on a topic, the pair must work to construct a joint list on which they agree, and prioritise this list. Allow a fixed time for this discussion and give the children a one-minute warning before the time is up.

Once the work has been completed, allow a short time for the class to discuss *how* they worked.

After the discussion, ask the children each to write down one aspect of collaborative work that they personally feel they are good at, and one aspect they feel they are not so good at.

If children are to value this work it is important that they see the results being used. You may choose to use photocopiable page 164 as the basis for a class discussion, as a questionnaire for other classes, or for individual pieces of writing.

4. Rules for collaborative work

Age range
Seven to twelve.

Group size
Pairs, groups of four and the whole class.

What you need
Rough paper, best-work paper, writing materials.

What to do
Begin by discussing briefly with the children which collaborative skills they found easy, and which they found hard. Pick up and extend any of the teaching points already made and introduce any others you feel are important. Then ask the children, working in pairs, to make a rough list (as long as they like) of 'Rules for collaborative work'. Allow 20 minutes for this.

Next, combine the pairs into groups of four. In this larger group, ask the children to collaborate to produce a single list for the group. This should be copied out and displayed on the wall.

5. Sharing ideas

Age range
Six to twelve.

Group size
Individuals and pairs.

What you need
Drawing paper, drawing materials, rough paper, writing paper.

What to do
Ask each of the children to invent and draw a magical creature that can help him or her with work at school. Explain that the children must produce a detailed drawing, because it will be used by another child as the basis for a piece of writing.

When the drawings have been completed, ask the children to swap drawings with someone else in the class. You can either tell them to swap with a friend or assign the children to pairs selected in advance.

Then allow the children two minutes *in silence* to carefully study the drawing they have received. There should be no discussion at all during this time.

Next, ask the children to write a character description of the creature in the drawing they have received, adding some imaginary details of their own – what it likes and dislikes, where it comes from, how it came about, where it goes at night, and so on. Make it clear that a detailed piece of writing is required. Only when the writing is finished should it be shown to and discussed with the monster's original creator.

Finally, discuss the work produced and the children's feelings about the activity. While some children will see that it can produce imaginative and inspiring results, others will find that it is not easy to allow treasured ideas to be altered by others.

You should encourage children to think in terms of shared responsibility for the outcome, and explore different ways of dealing with conflicting opinions. Some children will be pleased with the results, while others will not, and the class should recognise both the advantages and the disadvantages of this type of activity.

6. Making a story

Age range
Eight to twelve.

Group size
Pairs.

What you need
Rough paper, pencils, characters and descriptions from Activity 5, photocopiable page 165, blackboard or large sheet of paper.

What to do
You may need two sessions to complete this activity.

Tell the children that they are going to create a story in pairs, based on their work for Activity 5. Explain the task and the main storyline decisions that they will need to make. You should write the following information on a blackboard or a large sheet of paper so that it can be seen by all the children.

Task
One of the creatures you have invented appears for a day in school. You are going to write about what happens on that day.

Storyline decisions
• Which creature is it?
• How do you first become aware of it?
• Can everyone see it?
• Why did it come to your school?
• What adventure do you have with it on this day?
• Why does it leave?
• What happens in the end?

Things to think about

Remember, a story *must* be exciting. Keep rereading your story. Imagine that you are the child for whom it is being written.

Ask yourself:
• Is the story clear?
• Is it interesting?
• Is it exciting?

The task, the storyline decisions and the things to think about should be clearly displayed in the classroom until the end of the activity.

Tell the children that it is important for them to plan how they will work together. Explain how the storyline decisions can help with this and tell them that they will have 10 to 15 minutes to discuss and record their decisions. Emphasise that it is important for them to have sketched out and agreed the whole story by the end of this time. Their storyline decisions must be recorded in note form. Remember to warn them five minutes and one minute before the end of their discussion time.

You may find that the noise level rises during this task. Some children become excited and 'bubble over'; some have naturally loud voices and will need your help to moderate them. A pre-arranged signal which indicates to the class or to individuals that they should quieten down will often control the noise without destroying the atmosphere or interrupting the flow of ideas.

After the discussion time, give the children the paper on which they will write their rough drafts. Explain what is required for a first draft, and that handwriting, punctuation and spelling are not of paramount importance at this stage.

Show the children a sample of photocopiable page 165, on which they will write their final copy (when spelling, handwriting and punctuation will be important). Do not give out copies of this page yet. Discuss some of the ideas under the 'Things to think about' heading, and tell the children that these are the criteria on which their story will be judged.

Then the children can each write a first draft of the story, and allow their partners to read it when they have finished. Each child must find one thing she likes about the way her partner has told the story, and suggest one way to make it better.

Finally, both stories should be copied in best handwriting on to copies of photocopiable page 165. In discussing the work with the children, emphasise not only the content of the completed task, but also the collaborative skills used to produce it.

7. Building a travel agency

Age range
Eight to twelve.

Group size
Groups of four.

What you need
Large boxes, wallpaper books, carpet and material scraps, clear acetate film, small boxes, paints, felt-tipped pens, adhesive, sticky tape.

What to do
Children usually write easily when their ideas have been focused by a concrete experience.

Give each group a large cardboard box and ask the children to build a model travel agency. The group must make various decisions about the appearance of the agency, including where the front entrance should be, whether to have an awning and, if so, how to construct one. They can partition the box to make rooms, and decorate them using the carpet, wallpaper and fabric scraps. Windows can be made using clear film.

This activity requires plenty of time, and it is important that the children feel satisfied with the end product. It provides a rich opportunity for collaborating, talking and listening, design and technology, and problem-solving.

When the models are completed, with the name of the agency proudly displayed on them, the children can try the following writing task.

Ask the children to think about the behaviour of the group during the building of the model. Give them a sheet of paper with 'Good collaboration' written on one half and 'Bad collaboration' written on the other. They must think of incidents that happened during the model-building which are examples of good and bad collaboration. They should then elect two people to write a report on the collaboration, using this list of behaviours.

Meanwhile the other half of the group should write a set of instructions for making a model travel agency. The instructions should be numbered sequentially, and should be detailed enough to enable their model to be reconstructed by someone who has not seen it.

Finally, each group can show their model to the rest of the class and discuss the written work produced.

Further activity
See Activity 8.

8. Interview questions

Age range
Eight to twelve.

Group size
Groups of four.

What you need
Writing materials.

What to do
Tell the groups that they are to interview for a manager/ess to run the travel agency they have made in Activity 7 above.

Each group must discuss the sort of person they think would be good at such a job, and compile a list of desirable qualities, which should be written out by one member who has been elected the scribe.

Next, each member of the group must write two questions they would like to ask applicants for the job. Allow about four minutes to do this, and remember to warn the class when there is only one minute left.

The groups should then discuss all the individual ideas and make a final list of five questions to ask. You may need to emphasise that this could involve rewriting or combining some of the questions suggested.

Finally, each group member should individually write what he or she thinks would be the perfect response to each of the questions. The members of the group should compare and discuss these, and finish by taking one question each and writing the 'perfect answer', using ideas from all the responses.

9. Making a board game

Age range
Eight to twelve.

Group size
Groups of four.

What you need
Squares of card 5 × 5cm, large piece of card, colouring, drawing and writing materials, dice, counters.

What to do
Ask the whole class to discuss all the things that help and hinder good collaborative work in the classroom. These may include the ways in which the group members organise themselves, identify problems, discuss, listen to each other's ideas and stick to the task. The class should also consider how important it is for individuals

to help each other and to take responsibility for finishing their work and ensuring its quality.

Tell the children that each group is going to make a board game based on the idea of a group working together to achieve a particular task, such as tidying the classroom before the class party. Certain squares will be 'hot-spot' or 'crisis' squares, from which players can jump either forwards or backwards, depending on whether they draw a collaborative or a non-collaborative behaviour card.

The groups must discuss what sort of board game they will make. They will have to decide on an overall task which the players are endeavouring to achieve. The layout of the board must be discussed, along with details of how many players can play, how they will move, and how many 'hot-spots' there will be.

Group members should think of examples of good and bad collaborative behaviours which would hinder or help progress with the task, and write these on to the 5 × 5cm cards.

Once the game has been made, each member of the group should choose one of the following tasks:
• Write a list of rules for the game.
• Write the background story for the game.
• Write an advertisement for the game.
• Write a report on how the group collaborated to make the game.

The group's scribe should record who is doing which task.

Finally, the group should work together to display both the game they have made and also the pieces of written work produced by individuals in the group. Children in different groups should be encouraged to read and comment on each other's work.

10. Letters to a spy

Age range
Nine to twelve.

Group size
Individuals and the whole class.

What you need
Writing materials, envelopes, cardboard box.

What to do
Ask each of the children to choose a 'code name'. They must do this in secret and not tell *anyone*. Give them each a very small piece of paper and tell them to write their real name and their code name on it. These should be collected and stored in a sealed envelope. They are for your eyes only!

Tell the children that they have a special task. They will be told the code name of someone in the class, but they will not be told to whom it refers. They should not reveal to anyone which name they have been given. The task is to try to find five different ways in which they and their unknown partner are similar. The similarities can include anything: things they like doing, the sort of home they live in, the food or music they like, the comics they read and so on.

In order to find these things out, each child should write a two-paragraph letter beginning 'Dear fellow spy...' and signing off with their own code name. The first paragraph should be about themselves, revealing their likes and dislikes, but containing no details that would give their identity away. The second paragraph should ask questions, the answers to which might provide them with useful information when seeking similarities.

All letters should be put in an envelope, addressed with the code name of the unknown partner, sealed and placed in a special 'spy box'.

The following day, children should pick out the letter addressed to themselves, and write an answer. Again, these should be placed in envelopes, sealed and addressed in code before being placed in the 'spy box'.

The children can then claim their replies, and start compiling a list of similarities. If they cannot find five, they should write another letter. If they do find five similarities, they should display an open request in a specially designated place in the classroom, listing the similarities and asking their coded partner to come forward.

CHAPTER 2

Functional writing

Functional writing fulfils many practical purposes: letter writing; reporting; sending and replying to invitations; designing and filling out forms; writing lists; compiling instructions or directions. It includes any sort of writing that serves a practical function.

The purposeful nature of this writing makes a sense of audience essential. Knowledge of who the readers are and why they are reading will influence the whole nature of the writing; thus a letter written to a lawyer differs drastically from a letter written to a close friend.

Functional writing is the only type of writing that children will certainly have to do as adults. It is imperative, therefore, that they should be taught the conventions and allowed to develop their skills so that they will operate confidently and successfully in the adult world.

Too often children are given a formula for each type of functional writing, be it a letter or a report on a science experiment, and merely invited to apply the formulae in a succession of isolated, decontextualised situations.

There is nothing wrong with formulae – we suggest several ourselves in the following activities. However, they should not be the sole teaching input. To learn effectively, children must understand the links between the formulae and the reader's needs. They must understand why formulae work, and this involves discussion about who the reader is, what he or she needs to know and how best to order and structure the information to aid comprehension.

Common sense indicates that functional writing can only be taught within a context which makes the purpose clear for both the writer and the reader.

This chapter and the next are both about functional writing. This chapter describes situations which can be used to introduce a variety of functional writing activities to children of all ages. Chapter 3 identifies three contexts which offer rich opportunities for children to practise and develop functional writing skills.

ACTIVITIES

1. Invitation to a teddy bears' picnic

Age range
Five to six.

Group size
Individuals.

What you need
Writing materials, photocopiable page 166.

What to do
Teach the class to sing 'The Teddy Bears' Picnic'. Ask if they would like to have a picnic as a surprise for their own teddy bears. They are bound to say 'yes'!

With the class, make a list of all the things that will have to be organised for the picnic – invitations, food, drink, games and music. Show the children the invitation on photocopiable page 166 and go through it with them, discussing what could be written in each of the blank spaces. Each child in the class may invite a teddy bear or doll and bring it to school on the day of the picnic.

The day before the picnic, get the children to bring in some biscuits or crisps to share with everyone else. Make sure that any child who requires special food is catered for.

2. List of rules

Age range
Five to six.

Group size
Whole class.

What you need
Writing materials.

What to do
It is a good idea to do this activity when introducing a new activity or piece of equipment. Discuss how the equipment is to be used and tidied away, the maximum number of people who should use it at once, or how to work out whose turn it is. Talk about the reasons why it is important to have rules:
• to ensure the users' enjoyment and safety;
• to make sure that everyone has an equal opportunity to use the equipment;
• to protect the equipment.

Ask the children to suggest a way of reminding people of the most important rules for this particular piece of equipment. Take their suggestions seriously and discuss the feasibility of each. They may suggest writing or drawing a sign. Ask what the sign should say and write or draw the list in front of the class. Finally, display the sign near the equipment.

Further activities
• Ask the children what other signs or rules they can remember seeing (no smoking signs, road signs, rules at the swimming-baths and so on). Take the class for a walk around the school, looking at the signs and rules on display and discussing who reads them and what they mean.
• There are several stories about people who use signs. In particular, the children might like to read *Mrs Lather's Laundry* by Alan Ahlberg (Young Puffin).
• The children may like to make their own signs or rules for a piece of equipment or an activity with which they are familiar.

3. Recording information: running races

Age range
Five to six.

Group size
Groups of three, then individuals.

What you need
Space in which to run races, writing materials, flashcards saying 1st, 2nd, 3rd, first second, third.

What to do
This activity can also be used to consolidate maths work on ordinal numbers – first, second and third. The vocabulary could be introduced by first reading and then sequencing the story of *The Three Billy-Goats Gruff* with the class.

Divide the class into groups of three and take them into the playground. Once outside organise short running races and discuss who came first, second and third in each race. Return to the classroom and ask the children to draw pictures of their race as it finished. Emphasise that they must draw the children in the correct order. Underneath their drawings they could write simple sentences: 'I came third. Gill came first. Joe came second'.

Try to display the pictures and writing where parents, coming to collect the children at home-time, will see them. Write a big notice saying:

> PARENTS!
> Our class ran races today.
> Read this work to find out
> about your child's race!

4. Writing a list

Age range
Five to six.

Group size
Small groups.

What you need
Writing materials, a recipe or set of instructions for making something, ingredients and equipment, two or three willing adult volunteers.

What to do
Before you do this activity, it is important that you prime two or three adult volunteers who are willing and able to give the children the items on the lists described below.

Decide on a project such as making a cake or building a model, and tell the children what they are going to do or make. If possible, show them the written recipe or instructions, and read this with them so that they get a clear idea of what they will need and why. Give each child in the group some paper and a pencil, explaining that the first task is to gather together everything that is needed. Go through the instructions again, telling them to stop you whenever you mention an item that has to be collected. They should draw or write each new item as it is mentioned.

Divide the group into pairs or threes, and send them off to one of the adults from whom they can collect, unaided, a number of specific items from the list. (You could perhaps use the headteacher, the teacher of a neighbouring class, the school secretary or the caretaker.) The children should tick on their lists the items that they are to collect. Emphasise how important their list will be in reminding them of *all* the items! When the groups return, go through the lists and cross off the items collected. Then the group can make the cake or build the model as planned.

5. The class postbox

Age range
Five to seven.

Group size
Individuals.

What you need
Recent photographs of the children in the class (mounted with their names written clearly beneath), an additional 'flashcard' of each name, some letters sent to the school, a decorated cardboard box with a large 'posting hole'; writing materials, an ink-pad, a rubber stamp, old envelopes (if possible).

What to do
This is a good activity to do near the beginning of the school year. You can either send a letter home asking the children to bring in photographs, or take a few group photographs yourself to make the display. It is important that the children can be easily identified in the photographs, and their names easily copied from the display.

Begin the discussion by showing the children some of the letters sent to the school that day. Ask if they have ever received or sent a letter, and discuss the reasons why people might send letters, how they are posted and delivered and how it feels to receive a letter from a friend. Emphasise that a letter is special because you can look at it time and time again or put it up on the wall. It reminds you of the person who wrote it, even when they are not there. Writing a letter is a special act of friendship.

Show the class the postbox and explain that it is a special one, just for their class. They will be able to write a letter or draw a picture for anyone in the class, and post it. At the end of the day, the letters will be delivered. (You might like to nominate a 'postie' each morning.)

Encourage the children to write to a variety of people, not just to their best friend. Explain how important it is that they write their own name at the bottom of the letter or picture, so that the receiver knows who it is from, and that they write the name of the person to whom it is to be sent on the front of the envelope.

Demonstrate how to use the display to find out how to write the name. Emphasise that if the children copy from a flashcard, they should always take care to put it back in the right place.

You might like to start the activity off by getting the whole class to send a drawing or letter, or you may prefer to make it a genuine free-choice activity from the start.

6. Instructions for making sweets

Age range
Five to eight.

Group size
Groups of six to eight.

What you need
Ingredients and recipes for making a variety of sweets, writing materials, pictures of all the ingredients.

What to do
Start by telling the group which type of sweet they are going to make, what they will need and how they will make the sweets. Read the recipe with the children. While they are doing the cooking, emphasise the importance of the recipe book and help the children to identify the most important five or six parts of the process.

When the sweets have been made and the class has been given an opportunity to taste how delicious they are, ask the group whether they can remember exactly what they did. Take time to establish the sequence in which the children made the sweets. Point out that the children will eventually forget what to do, and also that other children in the class would probably like to make the sweets, yet might have difficulty reading the recipe book.

Suggest that the group share their knowledge of sweet-making by writing the recipe in a form that others in the class will be able to understand, with plenty of pictures to help. You may like to show them one of the published pictorial recipe books for children – but of course not one that gives the recipe for their particular sweet.

Give the group pictures of each of the ingredients to stick on to the first page of their book.

Give each child a sheet of paper which has been divided into four or six spaces. Ask them to think about the first thing they did and draw it, then the next, and so on. Emphasise that the drawings must show very clearly what was done at each stage. Underneath each picture, help each child to write a brief sentence which either gives

advice about the procedure in the picture, or explains it in further depth. Encourage the children to write a sentence which does *more* than simply describe the picture; text and pictures should both contribute to the instructions.

Each group should make a different type of sweet, and when all the groups have finished writing their recipes the children can compile them to make a book. Individual children can then browse through the recipe book and choose a type of sweet to make next time there is an opportunity to do some cooking.

Further activities
• When other children have followed the recipes in the books, you may like to discuss any problems they had, and talk about how the books could be altered, advice added or pictures clarified to prevent these or similar problems recurring.
• You might like to invite parents or older children into the classroom to try out the recipes in the books with a group of children.

7. An invitation to a special birthday

Age range
Seven to nine.

Group size
Individuals, pairs and the whole class.

What you need
Paper, pencils, drawing materials, sample invitations for birthday parties, christenings or naming ceremonies (the children could bring in their own).

What to do
Talk to the children about why they think people have birthdays and what their birthdays signify. Ask what they think happened on the day they were born. Remember that many of them may have had recent experience of a younger brother's or sister's

birth and naming ceremony. Ask them to find out what happened when they were born. What did their parents do and say? How did they choose a name, and how did they let others know about the new baby? Emphasise the number of different ways people can celebrate and remember the day a child is born.

Show them the invitations and discuss the information given inside. Is it all necessary? Why? Should anything else be added? Is it given in a particular order? Why are the most important pieces of information given first and often highlighted with larger, bolder writing?

Group the children in pairs and ask them to decide the most exciting way to celebrate the birthday of a child. Emphasise that anything is possible. Tell them that they are going to write an invitation to the celebration. Give them some rough paper on which to list all the important bits of information that people would need to know before they came.

When the pairs have made their decisions, ask each child to write an individual invitation. They do not necessarily have to write exactly the same thing as their partner, although the same core information will have to

appear on both. Ask the children to consider how best to use the style of script and the order in which information is given, to emphasise certain facts.

Once the children have written their invitations, they can decorate them.

8. Writing a letter

Age range
Seven to nine.

Group size
Individuals.

What you need
Official school writing paper with the school address shown at the top, envelopes, used envelopes, stamps (optional).

What to do
In order to establish that letter-writing is a two-way communication, it is important that the children are involved in a purposeful

correspondence with another person.

It is best if children write requesting information of some description, if they are to be assured of receiving a reply. Communication between two schools is a realistic and practical way of setting up correspondence between children.

Before introducing the conventions of letter-writing, ask the children to produce a rough draft to show what they actually want to say, which should be seen as the most important part of the letter.

Make the purpose of the letter clear to the children, whether it is to find out about life and routines in another school, to find out about individuals living in a different country or area or to find out about other children's opinions on particular issues.

Start by getting the children to write two lists; one of information that they feel would be of interest to whoever receives the letter, and one of questions they would like to have answered in the return letter. The first list can be used as a basis for the opening paragraphs, and the second to provide a structure from which the children can go on to compose the rest of the letter.

Before the children write a final draft of the letter, discuss with them the conventions of letter-writing. There is certain information that must be included to ensure a reply, and

the layout can help the reader to identify this information quickly. If headed writing paper is used, the child has only to place the greeting and opening sentence correctly on the page.

One of the most difficult features of letter-writing is addressing the envelope. Pin samples of used envelopes on the wall and discuss the different layouts for addresses. Many people now write addresses with one line directly beneath another, to give a straight left-hand edge. Point out how far down the envelope the name and address must start in order to leave room for a stamp and postmark. Ask the children to examine the envelopes on the wall, as well as those they receive at home, for good and bad examples of letter-addressing.

Letters must be stamped and posted. If children have access to a post-box, it is best if they can post them personally.

Further activity
If you have set the exercise up with another school, all the

children will receive replies. Give time for children to discuss and share their letters. Besides looking at content, examine the conventions used by other writers and use this as an opportunity to reinforce teaching points. The same format can be used for letters to pen-pals, and the content may be altered to suit thank-you letters.

9. Writing addresses

Age range
Seven to nine.

Group size
Individuals.

What you need
Photocopiable page 167, example of correctly laid-out letter and envelope.

What to do
This exercise will give children practice in writing addresses and addressing envelopes. It is advisable to have a large example of a correctly laid-out letter together with its envelope displayed on the wall to which the children can refer. Explain to the class how to address an envelope and letter-heading correctly.

Give each child a letter from photocopiable page 167.

Children must read the letters and then invent an address to put at the top of the sheet, and add a date and the names of the addressee and the sender, putting all this information correctly on to the letter. This is a good opportunity to discuss the basic structure of an address; the ways in which they vary and the ways in which they are all similar.

Further activity
Children should compare their own addresses, finding similarities and differences while noticing that there is a standard basic structure.

10. Newspaper announcements

Age range
Seven to nine.

Group size
Pairs or individuals.

What you need
Writing materials, typewriter or word processor, examples of the 'Birthday', 'Good wishes' or 'Celebrations' columns from local papers (enough for one example between two children).

What to do
Show the newspapers to the class and point out the announcements section. Give each pair a newspaper, and ask them to find the relevant section and draw a circle around all the announcements of birthdays and messages of good luck, congratulations and appreciation.

Ask the children to read out examples they have found. Do all the announcements say the same thing? Do they all include the same information?

Ask the children to write a short entry for this column, with a message for a friend in the class. They should do this in secret, without telling the friend for whom they are writing. If you have the facilities, their good wishes can be typed into a newspaper format and displayed in the classroom under an appropriate heading.

11. Model instructions

Age range
Seven to ten.

Group size
Individuals or pairs.

What you need
A model-making activity and the necessary equipment, writing materials.

What to do
You can either provide a whole-class stimulus for this activity by teaching the children a particular art and craft technique, or allow pairs of children to make a model of their own.

Once the children have finished the model, ask a colleague to come into the classroom, be impressed with the models and ask the children how they were made. Would her class be able to make similar ones? Suggest that the children could easily write some instructions which could be photocopied and given out to help the other class.

Begin by getting the children to write a list of all the things they did to make the model.

Each separate action should be written on a new line, and numbered to show the order in which they should be done. Once this is clear, tell the children to consider each instruction and add any warnings or advice to help with the particularly tricky parts.

It may help the children to clarify their ideas if you act as a naïve reader, asking basic questions where they have omitted details, and pointing out instructions which need to be clarified.

When the children are satisfied with their instructions, they can pass them on to the other class. Later, the children should be encouraged to visit those who used their instructions to see the results and find out how effective their instructions were.

12. Hidden treasure

Age range
Seven to twelve.

Group size
Pairs.

What you need
Photocopiable page 168, writing materials.

What to do
Give out copies of the plan of the castle on photocopiable page 168, and check that all the children have it the right way up, with north at the top of the page.

Explain that the castle is very big, and that some treasure is hidden in a secret room which is very hard to find; only you know where it is.

Ask the children to identify on the plan the different points at which they could enter the castle. Describe to the class a route from one of the entry points that would lead to the treasure. Ask the children to trace the route with their fingers as you do this.

Next, ask the children to do exactly the same exercise in their pairs, with one choosing where to hide the treasure and describing the route while the other traces it with a finger. They may need to try this several times with several different routes.

When the children can do this orally, ask them to write a set of instructions to say how to get to the treasure from a specified entry point. They could either do this individually, swapping to check instructions once they have finished, or as a pair, swapping instructions with another pair.

Further activity
Tell the children that they are prisoners in the dungeon of the castle and must write directions for each other to find their way out.

13. Menu for a monster's feast

Age range
Eight to twelve.

Group size
Individuals, then groups of four.

What you need
Drawing and writing materials, magazines and books on food.

What to do
Brainstorm with the whole class all the worst types of monster that they can think of. From this

list, each child should choose a monster without telling anyone else which one they have chosen. Then they must write a list of the types of food they imagine their monster would like to eat.

In groups of four, each child must describe his or her monster to the others in the group, saying when, where and what it likes eating. The group's task is to decide on the menu for a 'Monster feast', choosing the type of food, number of courses, and so on.

The group must discuss the best way to present all this information on the menu. The overall design of the menu must obviously be attractive to all the monsters, but it must also make certain information very clear. For example, how will they indicate that some foods are alternatives for the same course while others are a different course? What information will help monsters who are unfamiliar with certain dishes choose something they will like? Where should this information go?

Once the menus have been written and designed, they should be suitably decorated, mounted on card, and displayed in the classroom.

Further activity
This activity can form the basis of a piece of imaginative writing. The children will already have invented outline characters for their monsters, and the group can work together to invent and write the story behind the 'Monster feast' – the events leading up to it, what happened, and how it ended.

14. Designing a work record

Age range
Eight to twelve.

Size of group
Individuals or the whole class.

What you need
Writing materials.

What to do
If children are to learn to study effectively, it is important that they should know how to keep study records of work they have covered. Explain to the

children that for one week they are to keep a record of the tasks they carry out.

Discuss with the class the information that should be included on their record sheets. The list will probably include the following:
• the time each activity started and finished;
• a short description of each activity;
• the child's evaluation of the work;
• an evaluation of the child's personal level of satisfaction with the activity;
• space in which the teacher can comment on the child's work.

At the end of the week, ask the children to pin up their records, and discuss their clarity and the organisation of information. As a result of this session, children may wish to draw up a new kind of record form to use the following week.

Further activity

Children may later become involved in designing 'work planners' for planning and recording the work for a day or a week, or in designing records for specific activities.

15. Letter-writing

Age range
Nine to twelve.

Group size
Individuals.

What you need
Writing materials, paper, envelopes and stamps.

What to do
At the upper primary stage, children should be made aware of the difference between the language used in personal letters and that used in more formal letters. A formal letter requesting advice or information must be as brief as possible, stating only the facts that are absolutely necessary and requesting the information clearly.

To practise this, children might like to write letters to any of the following:
• organisations that can provide information for projects;
• authors, with queries about their books;
• television companies, requesting information about actors, programmes or particular backstage jobs;
• bus companies, to organise school trips;
• local companies or services, requesting information.

Begin by asking the children what information is absolutely *vital* in such a letter. They should produce a list something like the following:
• who you are;
• a description of the project in which you are involved;
• why the information is requested;
• a clear statement of what is required;
• a fairly formal ending expressing appreciation in advance.

The children should be told that a business letter to someone whose name is unknown is finished with 'Yours faithfully' and one to a person whose name is known ends with 'Yours sincerely'. The rule is never to put two 'S's (for 'Sir' at the beginning and 'sincerely' at the end) together.

Replies should be displayed in the classroom to reinforce the notion that important, busy adults take children seriously if they write thoughtful, careful letters.

The class will learn most about letter-writing by writing real letters and examining their replies. A display of replies which focuses attention on purpose and style will allow opportunities for teaching points to be reinforced during discussion, often by the children themselves.

16. Writing a police report

Age range
Nine to twelve.

Group size
Individuals, pairs and small groups.

What you need
Writing materials, a drama session on which the writing can be based.

What to do
Organise a drama session in which small groups of children invent and develop a conflict situation. For example, they might act out an argument between two people which escalates and a window is broken, whereupon an innocent bystander calls for a police officer, who interviews all concerned. The children in each group must decide:
• who the characters are and how they know each other;
• what the argument is about and how it started;
• how the conflict is resolved.

Each group must show their scenario to the rest of the class. Use this as an opportunity to draw attention to the role of the police officer. Try to encourage the children to think as deeply as possible about exactly what sort of facts he or she would need to establish: what exactly happened, what was said and by whom, the names of the witnesses, where they were standing at the time, and so on.

In the classroom, tell the children that they are going to write a police report concerning their group's incident. Discuss why such a report might have to be written and how it might be used. In pairs, get the children to brainstorm all the information that would need to be put into the report.

Before they write the report, the children will certainly need to discuss how to put the information into order, starting with the most basic facts. (Who? What? Where? When?) You may decide to ask the children to write separate reports, or to write in pairs. Once they are written, the reports should be shown to the other participants in the original drama scene for their comments.

17. Carnival costumes

Age range
Nine to twelve.

Group size
Individuals, then pairs.

What you need
Drawing, colouring and writing materials, prepared example of drawing-board designs and notes, example of fashion magazine description of clothes.

What to do
You will need two separate sessions for this activity.

First session
Talk to the class about why people wear special clothes for special occasions. Let the

children look at some magazines and books with pictures of clothes, and emphasise the variety of different ways to make the clothes special.

Ask the children to design and draw an outfit for a carnival. Show them how annotated drawings would be used to describe the original designs.

Ask the children to produce a drawing-board design of their outfit. Point out that it should be as original as possible. Emphasise that the written information on the drawing-board descriptions should be concise, and should add to the information shown in the drawings.

Finally, briefly discuss the way a fashion writer might describe the clothes, and ask the class to collect some examples of this type of writing before the next session.

Second session
Ask the children to form pairs and write a report on their partner's costume design as if they were fashion journalists. Remind them about how a fashion writer describes clothes, and allow them some time to read and discuss the language used in some of the examples that have been collected.

Give the children three minutes to look at their partners' annotated design drawings in silence. They may then have two minutes each to question their partners and find out as much additional information as possible.

Finally, they can write their reports. When these are finished, they can be shown to the original designer.

18. Recording results

Age range
Ten to twelve.

Group size
Pairs, then groups of eight.

What you need
Writing materials, magnifying glasses, clearly labelled samples of milk, cheese, tomatoes and bread which have been left for one week (a) on a heater; (b) in a fridge; (c) beside a window.

What to do
This activity is aimed at encouraging children to consider the advantages of different ways of displaying results. It should also help them to start questioning why food goes mouldy in different ways.

Group the children in eights, and then ask the group members to organise themselves into working pairs. Each pair must choose one sort of food to investigate, and collect the three samples. They should examine these carefully, describe what has happened and decide how this information could best be recorded. You may also ask them to consider why the things they describe have happened, and to write a short explanation.

The working pairs should then meet up as a group of eight. Each pair should report on their food in turn, showing the others how they chose to record what they found and why. Group members should be encouraged to comment on the advantages and disadvantages of each pair's method.

The group should discuss what happened to each type of food, whether it mattered where the food was left and whether each type of food reacted in the same way. As a group, the children should list as many different statements as possible about the different ways in which food can go mouldy. They can bring these suggestions, with their records and questions, to a class discussion.

Further activity
If they have not already done so, ask the children to do some close-observation drawings of the food samples studied in this activity.

An activity such as this one is obviously an excellent starting point for the children to plan an investigation into preservation and decay.

CHAPTER 3

Functional writing in a context

The activities in this chapter have been divided into three contexts for writing – 'Ourselves', 'Holidays' and 'Schools'. Each context has a strong story-line to guarantee involvement and response from the class, yet pin-points how particular activities might be used to target the teaching of particular writing skills.

The activities in the first section, 'Ourselves', are aimed at five- to seven-year-olds. They provide an opportunity for these children to look at human needs and characteristics.

The activities in the second section, 'Holidays', can be studied in the context of promoting the children's home town as a holiday resort, encouraging them to look at their local environment.

Finally, the third section, 'Schools', provides activities for producing a class newspaper and is aimed at nine- to twelve-year-olds.

All the activities suggested in these sections are vehicles through which the essential functional writing skills can be taught. They can either be studied as whole projects or as individual activities in their own right.

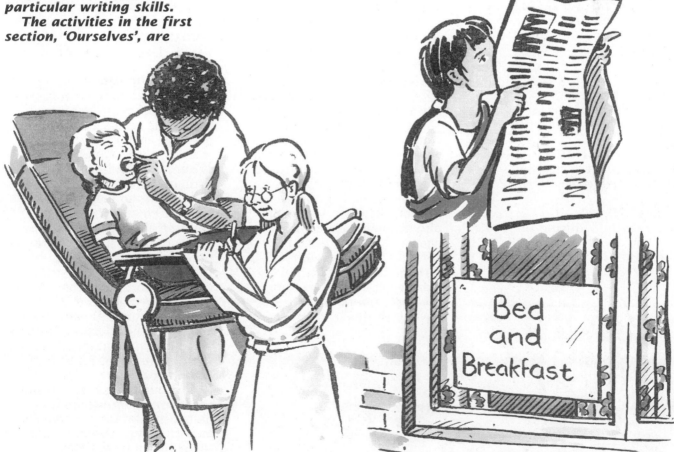

ACTIVITIES

Ourselves

The activities in this section give a chance to introduce these very important ideas to five- to seven-year-olds:
• that people have different needs;
• that people grow and change;
• that we all need to take care of ourselves and help each other.

1. Who am I? Making a quiz book

Age range
Five to seven.

Group size
Individuals.

What you need
Photocopiable page 169, writing materials.

What to do
Begin by introducing the game of 'Who am I?' to the class. Tell them that you are thinking of

someone special, someone in the class today. You are not going to say the person's name, but will describe him or her. When a class member *thinks* she knows who it is, she should silently raise her hand.

Start by describing the colour of the child's eyes, hair, skin, socks, shoes, pullover, skirt, and so on. Younger children may need some more explicit help initially, with both you and the class thinking aloud and working out who it could or could not be with each new detail, gradually narrowing the choice to a few children. The children will get the hang of this quite quickly and it is a good game for learning colour names, and developing concentration and the skills involved in listening and logical reasoning.

Explain that the children could play this quiz game whenever they liked by writing the details down. They could even invite other people to play the game with them.

Show the class a copy of photocopiable page 169 that has already been filled in to correctly describe yourself. Go through it, seeing if the children can guess to whom the sheet refers. When they have done this, explain how

they should fold and fill in their own sheet. Under the flap, the children should write their names and draw accurate self-portraits. Once the sheets have been filled in, they should be displayed around the walls of the classroom or made into a special book with the title 'Who am I?'

2. Looking after a baby

Age range
Five to seven.

Group size
Whole class and individuals.

What you need
Parent with a baby, display of baby food, magazines, toys, books and so on, writing materials.

What to do
Arrange for a parent with a young baby to bring the baby into the class and to talk to the children about how she or he looks after the baby. Ask the parent to emphasise the way the baby has changed since it was first born; perhaps by describing changes in physical appearance (hair, teeth and size of clothes), or by detailing the things the baby has learned to do since birth.

When asked, the children will be quick to suggest things that they can do which the baby cannot. Use this as an opportunity to discuss what the children were like as

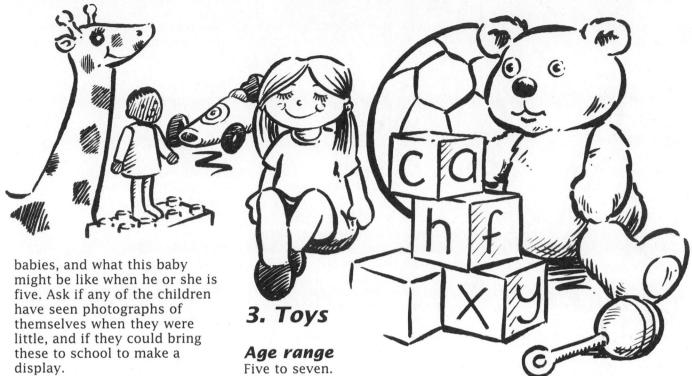

babies, and what this baby might be like when he or she is five. Ask if any of the children have seen photographs of themselves when they were little, and if they could bring these to school to make a display.

Ask the children to draw a picture of the baby, and to write:
• one thing that surprised them about the baby;
• one thing about caring for a baby.

When the children have done this, share the pictures and writing with the class. The work can then be mounted and made into a class 'baby book'.

Further activities
• Ask the children to choose a friend's work and, on another sheet of paper, do a drawing to illustrate what their friend has written about caring for a baby.
• After the visit, the class could write cards, pictures or letters to thank the parent for coming.
• Mount a display of the children's baby photographs and have a competition to see who can guess their identities.

3. Toys

Age range
Five to seven.

Group size
Individuals, pairs and the whole class.

What you need
Toy catalogues, adhesive, scissors, sheet of paper divided in half for each child.

What to do
Show the catalogues to the children and discuss the different types of toys. Give the children plenty of time to look at the catalogues and talk about the toys shown.

Help the children to write 'baby' on one half of their paper and 'my age' on the other, and tell them to cut out pictures from the catalogue and stick them on to the correct half of the page.

Have a 'sharing session' in which the children show their work to the rest of the class. Encourage them to comment on the decisions they made and why, emphasising that different age-groups require different things from a toy. The children should be able to explain how they recognise a toy that has been designed for a baby, linking this to the baby's needs and abilities.

The children should then help you to compile a class list to show what makes a good toy for a baby and what makes a good toy for children of their own age. You can also use this opportunity to discuss how the children judge a toy, and how they decide they have outgrown a particular toy.

Further activity
The children could be asked to draw a toy they would really like to own and a toy they do own, but no longer play with. Next to each picture, they should write the reasons why.

4. Making a game

Age range
Five to seven.

Group size
Individuals and the whole class.

What you need
Flashcards with words and phrases for children to discuss (such as 'feed myself', 'brush hair', 'get dressed', 'tie shoelaces', 'cross the road', 'cook', 'wash', 'brush teeth', 'make the bed', 'read a story', 'shop', 'wash clothes' and so on), paper headed 'Things we do for ourselves' on one half and 'Things others do for us' on the other, writing materials, blank flashcards.

What to do
This activity makes a good follow-up to a visit from a baby (see Activity 2, page 36). Remind the children about the baby's visit. Help them to remember all the things that a parent must do for a young baby, and emphasise that our parents once did these things for all of us.

Show the children the flashcards and the sheet of paper divided into two headings, 'Things we do for ourselves' and 'Things others do for us'. Discuss which flashcards belong under each heading. Invite the children to suggest some other things that they have learned to do for themselves and see if they can think of more things with which they still need help. Write their suggestions on the blank flashcards and put them under the correct heading.

Then give each child a sheet of paper divided into the same two sections. Make sure that they can read the headings. If the class is very young, appropriate drawings to illustrate each heading may help. Ask the children to pick the three most important things that they do for themselves and the three most important things that others do for them, and to use the flashcard words to help them write the words on their own sheets.

Once finished, the children should discuss what they have written and why. Eventually, they can use their sheets and the flashcards to play a simple word-recognition game. The flashcards are shuffled and the top one turned face-up. The children must try to match it to a word on their sheet of paper. The first child to match all the words on his sheet wins the game.

5. Clothes for all seasons

Age range
Five to seven.

Group size
Individuals.

What you need
Sack of clothes, photocopiable page 170.

What to do
Begin by discussing with the class what they each wore on their way to school that morning. Discuss whether this clothing was particularly suited to the weather conditions, and why. Ask who decides what clothes the children will wear each morning, and when and why this decision is made.

Show the children the sack of clothes, and tell them that they must guess what the weather was like when each item was worn. Ask why each item is suited to such weather; what would happen if it wasn't worn; how it protects the body from the wet, wind, cold or sun.

Show the children photocopiable page 170, and discuss the meanings of the four pictures. Tell the children to draw the clothes that they would wear in each type of weather in the correct quarter of the page, and to write a short sentence saying why.

Further activities
• The children can keep a personal weather chart, drawing pictures to show what the weather is like each day for two weeks. At the end of this time, older children can count the number of rainy days, sunny days, windy days, snowy days and so on, and show this information in the form of a bar chart.
• Read the children a story about the weather.

6. Visit to a clinic

Age range
Five to seven.

Group size
Individuals and the whole class.

What you need
A nearby dentist, health centre or baby clinic, a large pictorial map of the area (simplified if necessary), appointments book, record cards, writing materials.

What to do
When you contact the dentist, health centre or baby clinic to arrange the visit, explain that you are particularly keen for the class to learn about the different people working in the clinic, the jobs they do, and the sequence of events involved.

Before the visit, discuss what the children already know about the clinic: what it is for, who works there and what jobs they do. Encourage them to look at some of the many suitable books about visiting a clinic.

Show the class the map. Tell them to imagine that they are a bird flying over the area. As the bird looks down, it can see the school and it can see the clinic. Show the children where these are on the map. Ask what else the bird can see, and help the children to identify these places on the map, adding them in the appropriate place if necessary. Explain how the roads look on the map, and discuss the route you will take from the school to the clinic. Ask the children to trace the route with their fingers, and talk about what they will see along the way.

If the area and route are already familiar to the children, ask them to draw one thing that they will see on the way to the clinic. Then they can cut the picture out and, with help if necessary, stick it on to the map at the appropriate place.

At the clinic, emphasise the different sorts of writing that are necessary – appointment books, record cards, prescriptions, payment books and so on. If possible, let the children meet the people in the clinic who do this recording.

On their return to school, the children can do some of the following activities.
• Make a zigzag book showing the sequence of events when someone goes to the clinic. The children should be encouraged to make their drawings as detailed as possible and to discuss the sequence.
• Write a thank-you letter or do a drawing for the people in the clinic.
• Work in pairs to count their own teeth and fillings and to fill out a record card.
• Make the home corner into a clinic with an appointments book, a telephone, record cards, a waiting area and a treatment area. Encourage the children to use writing as part of their play.
• Trace the route to the clinic on the map and add further drawings of things the children saw on the way.

7. Playing safely

Age range
Five to seven.

Group size
Individuals and the whole class.

What you need
Large blank sheet of paper, smaller pieces of paper for the children, writing materials, large labels saying 'Safe places to play' and 'Dangerous places to play'.

What to do
Talk to the class about the different types of games they like to play, and list them on the large sheet of paper. Discuss where the best place to play these games might be. Some will need a lot of space, so discuss local facilities for this, such as parks and playgrounds. Do the children use these?

List all the different places in which the children play (gardens, roads, playgrounds, car-parks, building sites, bedrooms etc). Discuss the relative safety of these places, pointing out the hazards where necessary.

Ask the children to draw themselves playing, either in a safe place or in a dangerous place. They should not tell anyone which they are drawing. The drawings must be detailed, because other children will need to understand what they are playing and where.

When the drawings have been finished, collect the class together near the large labels saying 'Safe places to play' and 'Dangerous places to play', which should be stuck on the wall. Consider each drawing in turn, asking the children what is happening in the picture, and which label it should be displayed under and why. If any of the drawings are not detailed enough for the class to understand, the children should be asked to suggest further details which might help. The drawing can then be returned to its author for these to be added before it is placed with the correct heading on the wall.

Holidays

The area in which your school is situated may not seem an obvious place for people to come on holiday, but if you and the children search carefully, you will probably find that it has charms that are taken for granted by the local inhabitants. If your location really has no natural or man-made attractions, then the project could look at ways in which amenities could be improved in order to attract holiday-makers.

One project along these lines, entitled 'Advertising Lennoxtown as a holiday resort', we found to be very successful. Children began by canvassing opinions from recent visitors to the town. One disgruntled visitor described it as a 'one horse town', but another as the highlight of her holiday, the 'jewel of Caledonia'. The idea of a 'ghost-walk' (see page 45) was suggested by a child involved in that project. It proved a fascinating way of making local history come alive.

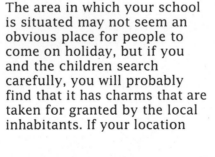

Dear Uncle George,
I hope that you are
well. Mum and Dad are well
and so am I although Susie
has a cold.
We are doing a
project in school ab...

1. Canvassing opinions

Age range
Seven to nine.

Group size
Individuals.

What you need
Writing materials.

What to do
Tell the children that they are going to advertise their town as a holiday resort. They must therefore find out if it is a good place for a holiday, and if not, what would make it so. To discover what people from outside think, they need to make contact with family or friends who have stayed in the area and ask for their opinion. Tell the class to go home and discuss this with their parents. If possible they should bring to school the next day the name and address of someone they could write to.

Most of the children will have someone to write to asking for opinions on the subject, but you could supply addresses for any who do not. There may be other members of staff who would be prepared to answer letters from some of the children. Alternatively, you could pair any child who does not have an address with someone who does.

Remind or teach the children about the conventions of letter-writing and addressing envelopes.

Help them to structure their letters by writing the following reminders on the board:
• Ask the person how he or she is.
• Tell him or her a little bit about your family and how you are getting on.
• Explain about the project you are doing in school.
• Ask if they will reply, telling you what they feel your town has to recommend it as a holiday resort or what improvements they feel should be made to it.
• Finish with best wishes.

Ask the children to put their home addresses on the letters, rather than the school address, so that they will have the thrill of experiencing a reply at first hand.

When the letters have been written and envelopes addressed, the children could either buy a stamp from you or provide their own. It is important that each child posts his or her own letter. Either take the whole class for a walk to the post-box, or let the children post their letters on their way home from school, having first ascertained that they know where the nearest post-box is. This may be the first letter that some children have written, and posting the letter will enhance their pride of ownership.

It has been our experience that most adults respond warmly to these requests. Some children may not receive replies, but although they will be disappointed, at least they have gone through the important process of sending a letter.

When the replies arrive, either you or the child concerned can read them to the class. They can be mounted as a display, under the heading 'What visitors

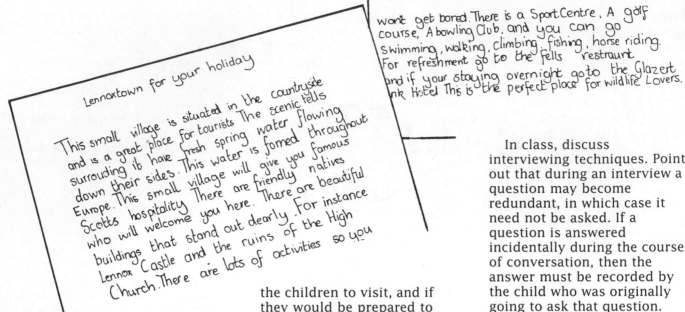

Lennoxtown for your holiday

This small village is situated in the countryside and is a great place for tourists. The scenic fells surrounding it have fresh spring water flowing down their sides. This water is formed throughout Europe. This small village will give you famous Scotts hospitality. There are friendly natives who will welcome you here. There are beautiful buildings that stand out clearly. For instance Lennox Castle and the ruins of the High Church. There are lots of activities so you wont get bored. There is a Sport Centre, A golf course, A bowling Club, and you can go Swimming, walking, climbing, fishing, horse riding. For refreshment go to the fells restraunt and if your staying overnight go to the Glazert nk Hotel This is the perfect place for wildlife Lovers.

think of our town'. When all the replies have come in, the children can use the information received to write an advertisement for the town, or a set of proposals for turning it into a more attractive place to visit.

2. Interviewing local managers

Age range
Seven to nine.

Group size
Individuals and small groups.

What you need
Writing materials, clipboards, tape recorder, camera (if possible).

What to do
Find five or six local amenities that tourists would use in your area, such as shops, clubs, hotels, restaurants, sports centres, coffee bars and libraries. Ask the managers of these places if they will allow the children to visit, and if they would be prepared to answer questions about their establishments. It is a good idea to contact parents and arrange for small groups to visit one place each, but if all else fails, take the whole class on one visit yourself.

Tell the children what you have arranged, and explain that after the visit they will be asked to make a brochure to describe and advertise the place they have visited. In order to do this, they will have to find out as much information as possible. To help the children focus on the place they will be visiting, ask each group to think of some questions in advance.

First of all, working individually, the children should each write five questions requesting information that they feel visitors would want to know.

In their groups, the children should then discuss the questions and write a composite list. They can share out the questions so that each child will be asking and recording the answers to a few questions.

In class, discuss interviewing techniques. Point out that during an interview a question may become redundant, in which case it need not be asked. If a question is answered incidentally during the course of conversation, then the answer must be recorded by the child who was originally going to ask that question.

If a camera is available, the children could take photographs, as long as they have first obtained permission from the relevant manager.

Further activity
The children could practise by interviewing classroom visitors. The interviews could be written up for a 'holiday brochure'. Possible subjects for interview could include 'Our local PC'; 'A famous person who lives in our town'; and 'Our sports centre manager'.

3. Making a brochure

Age range
Seven to nine.

Group size
Individuals, small groups or the whole class.

What you need
Card, writing paper, photographs or sketches from the visit in the previous activity, adhesive, scissors.

What to do
Explain to the class that they are to make a brochure advertising the place that they visited. They should use their original interview questions as headings under which to organise the information in the brochure.

In groups, the children must decide:
• How should the questions be ordered?
• Should the questions be re-phrased for the brochure?
• What information needs to be added?
• How will they avoid duplicating information in their answers?

Having made these decisions, each child in the group should take responsibility for a number of questions. They should write the headings and then summarise the information, mounting relevant photos and drawings. Finished work should be filed in a clean box or drawer ready for the final paste-up.

When all the work is finished, it can be organised into a book. Details of how to do this are given in Chapter 10.

Further activity
When they have been displayed for a suitable length of time in the school, these brochures could be sent to the places they advertise. Most local hotels and restaurants will be pleased to display this sort of information for their guests to read.

4. Advertising bed and breakfast

Age range
Seven to nine.

Group size
Individuals, small groups and the whole class.

What you need
Bed and breakfast brochures, photographs or drawings of the children's homes.

What to do
Ask the children if they feel there will be sufficient accommodation in the area for the many tourists who will pour in as a result of their advertising campaign. Suggest that the children could perhaps find space in their own homes to offer bed and breakfast. It may involve children in doubling up with brothers or sisters, or sleeping in a tent in the garden or park, but they will surely find a room if they try!

Form the children into groups and give each group a few brochures. Ask the children to note the ways in which 'B & B' is advertised. Point out the persuasive language used, and ask the children to quote examples of this from their group's brochures. Remind children that this is the sort of exaggerated language they will have to use in advertising their own home for bed and breakfast.

Look at the symbols used to indicate amenities offered, and ask the children to use these.

Can the children think of symbols that would show facilities attractive to children, such as toys provided, a boy of nine to play with, a sandpit in the garden or trees to climb? The new symbols invented to represent these facilities must be clear.

Each child should write an advertisement for his or her own home. Children will need a photograph or a drawing of the house to go with this. In Walthamstow, where all the children lived near the school, one teacher took her class and camera on a 'grand photographic tour'. The children had to plan the route in advance so that all the houses were visited in a logical order. They each took a photograph of their own house!

Many teachers have been pleased and surprised at the interest shown by parents when the bed and breakfast brochures are displayed.

5. A breakfast menu

Age range
Seven to nine.

Group size
Individuals.

What you need
Pieces of A4 card folded in half, writing and colouring materials.

What to do
Discuss with the children what they think the visitors staying in their houses would expect to have for breakfast. They should find out from the class how much they know about breakfasts eaten in other countries. What about people on special diets? If possible, it might be a good idea to show the class some books on this subject.

Each 'B & B' will have to offer two breakfast menus. These should be worked out in rough and then written beautifully on to the two inside pages of a piece of A4 card which has been folded in half. The front of the card should be decorated with the name and logo of the 'B & B' establishment.

The finished menus can then be displayed alongside the 'B & B' advertisements.

6. Directions to a place of interest

Age range
Seven to nine.

Group size
Individuals and pairs.

What you need
Local street map, enlarged and photocopied; writing materials.

What to do
Explain to the class that 'B & B' guests will need clear directions to get from where they are staying to local places of interest. Ask each child to choose one place of interest on the street map and to write how to get to that place from their house. The directions must be written unambiguously, with each new direction on a new line. Once these have been written out, the children should swap them with a partner for checking.

The children will need to be taught a way of remembering which is right and which is left, and how this relates to the direction of travel.

Further activity
The children could devise a tour of the area, working out an itinerary which includes three interesting local places.

7. A souvenir book

Age range
Seven to nine.

Size of group
Individuals and the whole class.

What you need
Small plastic bags, A4 sugar paper.

What to do
Show the class some examples of mementoes which you have collected while on holiday – a pressed flower from Switzerland, a shell from the beach, a piece of rock from Calvary or a stone from the Ganges. Encourage the children to tell the class about any such mementoes they have themselves. Ask them to think of examples of interesting things in their area which could be collected as mementoes.

Give each child a small plastic bag, and ask them to find something special to place in it. They must be given a deadline for finding their mementoes; a week, for example, would give time for flowers to be pressed.

When the time is up, ask the children to staple the plastic bags containing their exhibits on to one half of an A4 piece of sugar paper. On the other half, the children should stick a description of the memento. Write headings on the board for this:

• place of collection;
• time of collection;
• date of collection;
• description;
• why this is important and special;
• name of contributor.

The completed mementoes could be displayed on the wall, and later placed in a ring-binder with the title 'Our memento book'.

Further activities
• Each child could be asked to sketch their memento in detail or to speak for one minute about it to the class, justifying it as a truly interesting specimen.
• The children could make a recipe book of favourite local foods for visitors to take home.

8. A ghost-walk

Age range
Seven to nine.

Group size
Four to six.

What you need
A place nearby with an eventful history, writing materials, responsible adults to supervise.

What to do
Many Heritage Centres arrange 'ghost-walks' around places which are associated with past dramatic events or legends. Try to find an interesting old building, church or graveyard as near to your school as possible. This will obviously

depend on the location of your school, but remember that many 'new towns' have been built over old farms or villages, and new schools are often built near the site of an older one. In this case, the headteacher's diaries, punishment books and records relevant to the old school may still remain as a source of evidence.

Begin by asking the children if they have ever been on a ghost-walk when on holiday, and if so, to explain the idea to the class. Tell them that each group is going to devise a short ghost-walk for visitors to their town. The assembly point will be the school. The children will have to walk the visitors to the place and, once there, tell them its story. Parents, the headteacher, school governors and other adults could be asked to go on the ghost-walks.

Tell the children about the place nearby that you have identified, and tell them the story that goes with it. Each group should appoint a scribe to take down the story, with the others adding the details.

Several days later, get each group to read their version of the story out loud to the rest of the class. Make sure that each story has plenty of details to give as much colour as possible. These completed stories will be used as the scripts for the group's ghost-walk, and should be copied or typed neatly.

Give the children an opportunity to practise reading the script with as much expression as possible. Then each group should choose one or two readers who will tell the tale in the actual location in which the events took place.

Explain to the children that each group must decide who will be invited to their ghost-walk. It is best to specify the maximum number of guests, and at least one adult who will be responsible for the group.

The group must then decide:
• who will write the invitations;

• who will make a poster to advertise the walk;
• who will draw the illustrations for the story, and how many such illustrations there will be.

Each pair in the group should have a task to do that will help in arranging the ghost-walk.

Put aside a whole morning or afternoon for the walks. Help the children to decide whereabouts in school people will meet, and work out a timetable so that groups will not overlap.

On the day of the ghost-walk, organise work to allow the groups to leave and return at different times. Explain the work to the children the day before, and write it on task-charts or on the board to remind them. Children must be clear about what they have to do before and after their ghost-walk. Remember that the children will be excited on returning to the classroom, and it may be wise to discuss in advance how you expect them to behave.

Further activities

Ask the adult ghost-walkers to respond in some concrete way to the experience, either by writing a short letter or by visiting the class to say thank you.

If circumstances permit, you can give each group a different location and story and do the ghost-walk as a class, with each group telling its own story to the others and, of course, to the visitors.

Schools

Producing a class newspaper is an exciting and meaningful way for nine- to twelve-year-olds to study the school and the local community. Essential language skills are learned almost incidentally, and the children seem to blossom with a sense of responsibility and importance. They stride purposefully around school, clipboard, camera and tape-recorder in hand, carrying out the job of reporter for the class or school newspaper.

Technology also takes on a new meaning. Cameras, tape-recorders and computers are no longer things to play with, but are dynamic aids to the work of a writer.

The activities suggested are vehicles through which essential functional writing skills can be taught. Many ideas from other parts of this book can also make excellent newspaper copy. It would, for example, be possible to have a poetry page using ideas from Chapter 8.

A vist from a journalist

To produce a newspaper, the children must first know how to write a report. In this chapter we suggest some activities which can be used to teach children to do this, but these are weak substitutes for a visit from a real journalist. Local newspapers are generally delighted to raise their profile in the community by sending a reporter into school. A journalist who has practical experience of the reporting process can explain the structure of a report in a clear and straightforward way, and the children will thrive on the experience of being taught to write by a real writer.

There are three aspects of journalism in particular on which you could ask your visitor to focus:
• how to write a report;
• how to 'paste up' a newspaper;
• what a reporter's life involves.

To get the maximum benefit from the experience, the children should prepare some questions to ask before the journalist visits.

Organising the classroom

Making a class newspaper is a dynamic and memorable experience for children and teachers, but it calls for careful class organisation. All the routines for collaborative groupwork must be established (see Chapter 3).

It is essential to set up a filing system for completed and ongoing work. This can consist of:
• A4-sized trays which can be set out on work surfaces or stacked;
• cardboard or plastic folders that have been stapled to the wall;
• work-card holders which have been relabelled.

Whatever filing system is devised, the children must know how important it is to file their work accurately. To help them, containers *must* be clearly labelled with the subject matter and status of the work, for example:
• 'INTERVIEWS WITH TEACHERS (Rough drafts)';
• 'INTERVIEWS WITH TEACHERS (Finished print-outs)'.

Organising the children

It is helpful to introduce an ongoing individual project before beginning work on the newspaper. This gives children alternative work to which they can turn at all times. Alternatively, they can make a 'Book about me', which, by its nature, demands that children work alone without relying on the teacher. If you do this, it is sensible to provide a list of suggestions or titles such as 'My favourite menu', 'Four things I hate to eat', 'My best friend', 'Three wishes for my family', 'My joke page' and so on. Make Banda sheets with headings and instructions to help motivate the children and structure their work.

Dividing the tasks

After working on Activity 2 or 3 (pages 49 and 50), you may like to split the class into editorial teams, each responsible for a different area. Each task may then be presented to the relevant team. Alternatively, you may ask that each task be done by all groups in the class, with the best result chosen for publication.

Organising the technology

It will be essential to have a computer in the classroom at all times during the newspaper project. Enter into a deal with your colleagues and try to gain monopoly of it for three or four weeks, as once you start, the computer will be in use for most of the day.

The cost of the project

Some headteachers look upon a newspaper project as being so rich in language and environmental experience, and such a good advertisement for their school, that they are prepared to bear the burden of production costs. Other teachers feel that producing a cost-effective newspaper is part of the learning experience. By taking adverts for local businesses and charging for the newspaper, the class can certainly cover the cost of paper and photocopying.

Introducing a time limit

It is a good idea to introduce a time limit, as for a proper newspaper, and give a publishing deadline at the start of the project. Three or four weeks is ample time in which to produce a substantial newspaper. Some teachers suspend the normal curriculum for that time, turning the classroom into a newspaper office. Others prefer to keep the normal curriculum going each morning, leaving the afternoons free for uninterrupted newspaper work.

1. Brainstorming a newspaper

Age range
Nine to twelve.

Group size
Groups of four to five.

What you need
Adhesive, rough paper, writing materials, large sheet of paper, newspapers.

What to do
Give two folded newspapers to each group of children. Explain that the class is going to make a newspaper about the school. To do this, they must be aware of the types of articles that appear in newspapers. Without looking at the papers, the children should brainstorm the articles they might expect to find. Children will mention both categories of articles and discrete subjects. Show them how to group subjects under collective headings, for example:

SPORT:
>Football
>Tennis
>Racing
>Cricket

ENTERTAINMENT:
>Television listings
>Films
>Forthcoming events

When they run out of ideas, ask the groups to find some more by looking through the newspapers they have been given.

After this, give each group five to ten minutes to brainstorm ideas for things that people may be interested in reading about the school. The children should organise these ideas into the categories used for the first brainstorm. Some groups may be slow to get going, and you may find that it is necessary to throw out a few suggestions; for example, 'FASHION: School uniform – What do parents, children and teachers think?'

As with all brainstorms, it is important to allow the children total freedom in their ideas, to encourage originality and diversity. Not every idea will be used. Remember to warn the groups four minutes and one minute before the end of the activity.

Each group must elect a spokesperson to explain the results of the brainstorm to the rest of the class. The brainstorms must then be displayed on the wall for a few days, where people can reach them and add any additional ideas which may occur to them. (This, of course, includes you.)

Explain that these brainstorms will eventually be used to organise the paper. However, a period of time between the brainstorm and the actual organisation gives both you and the children an opportunity to reflect on possibilities.

In the end, you may choose to allocate areas randomly to groups, or you may allocate specific ideas to specific groups, allowing those who thought of particular ideas to work on them.

2. Writing a report

Age range
Nine to twelve.

Group size
Individuals and the whole class.

What you need
Photocopies of *carefully chosen* newspaper reports, writing materials, photocopiable page 171.

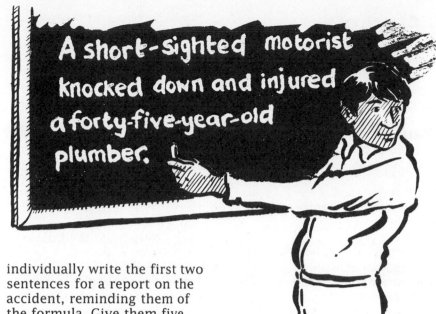

What to do
Explain to the class that reports are written to a very clear formula. People reading a newspaper want to know the news immediately, and so the first sentence must indicate what the whole report will be about. The next few sentences should give all the essential information. This is sometimes referred to as the 'five Ws': Where, What, Why, Who and When. Having read the most important facts, people can then choose whether or not they wish to read on for a more detailed elaboration of events.

Give each group a different report. (Make sure that you have first checked your examples to see that the formula works!) Ask each group to identify and underline the important information in their report. Ask them to identify the first three sentences of their report and to list the essential information contained in these. Ask a couple of groups to share their examples with the rest of the class.

Give out copies of photocopiable page 171, which shows the story of an accident. Tell the children to individually write the first two sentences for a report on the accident, reminding them of the formula. Give them five minutes to do this, and then ask some of the children to read out their ideas. Write these on the board. Check with the class that they fulfil the formula requirements, and ask for suggestions for improvements. This process illustrates the procedure of drafting and redrafting to find the most satisfactory opening for the report.

Next ask the children for suggestions about further details or information readers might wish to know about the accident. Point out that journalists like to have quotations from an eye-witness or person involved, and that often these people are described by an adjective before the name, for example, 'worried Mr Brown...' or 'angry motorist, Peter Matthews...'.

Tell the children to finish their reports. Allow them to use either the opening sentences on the board or their own. Specify a maximum and a minimum length to encourage them to think about how to report information in a concise way.

The skills introduced in this activity are the essence of effective report writing. The teaching points will have to be made several times in several different contexts. Organising information and structuring a report are complex skills which can only be developed through practice.

Children should practise these skills within the complete process of writing a report, and also by considering different aspects in isolation. For example, they could:
• identify important information in reports written by others;
• list and prioritise important information concerning real life events;
• produce just the opening sentences of a report;
• write a report on the basis of a given opening sentence and prioritised list of information;
• choose the best opening sentence from several suggestions and justify their choice.

3. Market research

Age range
Nine to twelve.

Group size
Individuals, groups of four or five or the whole class.

What you need
Writing materials, graph paper.

What to do
Discuss the problem of paying for the paper and photocopying which are necessary to produce a newspaper, and ask the children to think of ways of raising this money. They will probably come up with the idea of selling the paper, but they must also be encouraged to consider the notion of selling advertising space in the paper.

It will be necessary to work out the approximate length of the paper, and to estimate how much it would cost to produce. This can be done in groups or as a class. Ask each group to suggest four different cover prices for the paper, remembering that some money will be raised through advertising. Pool the suggestions, and get the whole class to vote and agree on four possible cover prices to investigate.

Each group must then choose, or be allocated, a different section of the potential readership to investigate. Explain that they have to find out how much each would be willing to pay for this high-quality paper. The sections chosen might include particular classes, other teachers, the lunch-time staff, the parents, the cleaners and so on. The questions should ask if people would be 'very likely', 'quite likely', or 'not at all likely' to buy the paper at the various cover prices suggested.

Each group must consider how to introduce and explain their questions. They will need a short introduction to read to the participants. This should consist of just a few lines to explain why the information is needed and to give clear instructions about the choices and how to respond.

Although this is only a short piece of writing, most children find it quite difficult to write instructions that are both clear and concise. For this reason, it is best to ask each child to produce an individual piece of writing, which should be shared either with the whole group or with one other person (depending on how good they are at collaborative work). The writing should then be modified and the best example chosen.

Finally, the group must decide how the various choices can be clearly and logically laid out, with enough space left to record the responses.

Each group should record its results as a bar chart. Finally, the children should work in pairs to write a report of the results (using the formula mentioned in Activity 2, page 49) and recommend a price for the paper. These suggestions can be duplicated and used as a basis for discussion, if there is disagreement between the groups.

4. Selling advertising space

Age range
Nine to twelve.

Group size
Pairs.

What you need
Writing materials, envelopes.

What to do
The idea of selling advertising space has already been introduced. The problem is now to find local shops or companies who would like to commission an advertisement in the paper. Ask the children to form pairs and decide whom they think might like to advertise in the newspaper. Compile the suggestions into a class list to ensure that letters will not be duplicated.

Remind or teach the class the conventions of letter-writing. For this letter, it is advisable to use the school address. Discuss with the class the content of the letter and write the main ideas on the board, giving them a structure to work to:
• an opening explanation about the class newspaper;
• an explanation of the need to sell advertising space;
• some reasons why it might be a good idea for the people contacted to advertise;
• a sentence asking them to advertise and explaining the

design service and the cost;
• the promise of a free copy of the newspaper;
• a polite signing off.

The children should be asked to write ideas for the letter in pairs, and one child can write the letter in rough.

They must understand that this is a very formal letter, and that the language, spelling, punctuation, handwriting and layout must be perfect. After all, who would want to advertise in a newspaper that is likely to be untidy or full of mistakes? After making corrections, the second child must copy the letter in neat handwriting.

It is advisable with any letter of this sort to sign your own name under the children's. If children take the letter to the business premises and ask for a snap decision from the proprietor or manager (collecting the money on the spot) it produces a much better response rate. Having to make a reply and send it by post involves more work on behalf of the business.

When money for advertising is received, you should send a receipt and a short note of thanks. It is imperative that anyone contributing should receive a free newspaper and further thanks for their help at the end of the project.

5. Writing an advertisement

Age range
Nine to twelve.

Group size
Pairs or the whole class.

What you need
Newspapers with advertisements, black felt-tipped pens, rough and good quality white paper cut to advertisement size.

What to do

Ask each pair to choose an advertisement from the newspapers. Point out that some words are in bold print, some are in capitals, and some in small letters, and ask the children to find examples in the advertisements they have chosen.

Discuss why the words are in different sizes and types of print, why some advertisements are illustrated and why some have fancy borders.

Ask the pairs of children to decide what information people need to know about the company, shop or amenity they are advertising. They should write the information as a list and then prioritise it. This information should then be put into the form of an advertisement, emphasising the most important details.

Children should be encouraged to quickly outline a number of different designs in rough, until they are satisfied that a particular design looks attractive, is eye-catching and contains appropriate information. This design should then be produced carefully, using black felt-tipped pens on good quality paper. Discuss why only black pen is used (the reason is that other colours do not photocopy well).

Further activity

The same process can be used to produce posters advertising the newspaper.

6. Planning a competition

Age range
Nine to twelve.

Group size
Groups of six.

What you need
Writing materials.

What to do

It is the process of writing clear and precise rules and instructions that is important for this activity.

Ask each editorial team of six children to decide on a competition which will be included in the paper. For instance, they might consider asking readers to submit designs for a new school logo or uniform.

Before beginning this task, list on the board all the decisions that the children must make in their groups.
• Who will be eligible to enter the competition? If the whole school is to be involved, consider splitting the age-groups and judging them separately.
• How is the competition to be judged, and who will do this? It may need to be done in stages, with perhaps the editorial team judging the first round, but a 'prestige' person judging the finalists.
• What will be the prize?
• How will the winner be publicised?

The final decisions must be written down by the group. The questions provide a structure for the writing.

Once the decisions have been made, each group of children should describe their competition and write out the rules.

7. The hobbies page

Age range
Nine to twelve.

Group size
Individuals.

What you need
Writing materials.

What to do

Ask the children to think about their favourite hobby. Explain that they are going to write about this for the newspaper, and their report might encourage others to share their pleasure and take up the hobby themselves.

Begin by asking the children to write down all the ideas that come into their head when they think of their hobby and why they enjoy it.

Then they can use these ideas to write two short paragraphs – one on what their hobby is like and one on why they enjoy it. Tell them to imagine that they are talking to someone who knows nothing about their hobby and to write a list of instructions to explain it. Emphasise that the sentences should be short, clear and to the point. Finally, they should describe how a newcomer might take up the hobby.

Further activity
Children could use their brainstorm ideas to make a poster to advertise their hobby.

8. Reviews

Age range
Nine to twelve.

Group size
Individuals.

What you need
Writing materials, reviews of children's books.

What to do
Explain that reviews are written by people who are considered experts in their field. Others read their opinions and often decide to see a film or television programme or read a book on the basis of the review.

First, show the children some of the reviews you have collected. Read them aloud, and ask the children to decide how they would react on the basis of each one. Would they want to read the book? Explain

that it is easiest to write a review by concentrating on the parts that are either very good or very bad.

Each individual must choose a book, film or television programme to review. They should then:
• write one sentence that sums up their feelings about the piece;
• write a couple of sentences to describe it;
• write a couple of sentences to describe its mood;
• write a couple of sentences to describe its pace;
• describe the most interesting characters;
• describe the best or worst part, and say why they felt this way about it;
• write a couple of sentences to say what type of person would enjoy it.

All these initial responses may need to be rewritten several times before the children feel they are exactly right for inclusion in the final review. Ask the children to look at the way the sentences flow together, and to check that the language is in keeping with the reviews the children have read.

Further activities
Reviews can be written for local events, school matches, class publications or books, school dinners, assemblies, or even lessons.

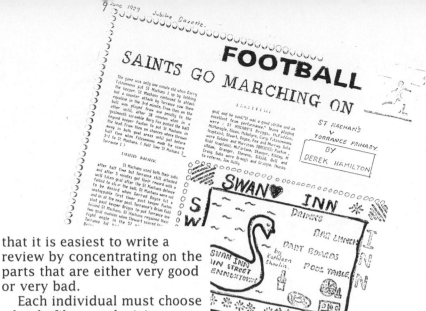

9. Letters to the editor

Age range
Nine to twelve.

Group size
Individuals and small groups.

What you need
Writing materials, letters pages from local or national newspapers and children's magazines.

What to do
Give each group of children the letters pages of various local and national newspapers and children's magazines. Ask them to list the issues raised in the letters, and collate these on the board, noting that letters often refer to previous articles or letters in the newspaper, and that people do not always want to complain when writing; sometimes they wish simply to point something out.

Then ask one member of each group to read out the

appropriate for them to write to the Local Education Authority, expressing their concern and asking further explicit questions.

most interesting letter in that group's sample, and use this to highlight the tone and style of letters to the editor. They should note the different ways of signing off – 'Yours with concern', 'Yours angrily', 'Yours in hope', and so on.

Ask each child to think of an issue relating to school or the local community and write a letter to the class newspaper.

All the letters should be displayed on a board, and the children can respond to each other's letters if they wish. Pin their replies on top of the original letters and look out for letters which receive no reply. You could respond to these yourself. It can also be great fun to ask an adult with a good sense of humour to reply to some of the letters.

The editorial team can then choose the most interesting sets of letters and publish both the originals and the responses.

Further activity
If the children raise major issues, for example vandalism or school hours, it might be

10. Star spot

Age range
Nine to twelve.

Group size
Groups of two or three.

What you need
Writing materials.

What to do
Each group must decide on a person in the school or the community who has been particularly successful recently in some way, or who helps the children regularly, but is rarely thanked. It might be the highest scorer in the school team, the crossing patrol person, the school cook, or a prominent local person.

First, the children should list all the things they wish to know about the person, in order of priority. They should then discuss how to find out this information. If they need to interview the person, they will have to decide:
• How will they arrange the interview, and where and when will it be conducted?

• What questions will they need to ask?
• Who will take responsibility for which questions?

Once this has been decided, the children should report to you, detailing their questions and plans. At this stage, anything that is not acceptable should be vetoed.

Once the interview has been carried out, the children will need to write a collaborative profile of the person. They should discuss the information they have, and decide if the order of priorities which was established earlier needs to be changed.

Each child should take responsibility for writing a short paragraph on the person, concentrating on their own questions. The final report can be presented with a large star and a photograph of the person in question.

Further activity
People profiles can be written for any section of the newspaper. The pets page could feature the local vet, the fashion page could carry an interview with the owner of a local fashion shop, and so on. A profile of a famous person for the general interest page will involve the children in researching the information they need from books and magazines. A letter should be written informing the person profiled that he or she has been featured in the class newspaper, including a copy of the paper.

CHAPTER 4

Imaginative writing

Children love the world of the imagination. From early infancy they respond to stories, cartoons and films. We are all familiar with the long stories told by very young children as they slip with ease into fantasy. It is vital that we harness this ability and love of story-telling and use it in the teaching of writing. Imaginative writing involves children in taking a step beyond real experiences into a world of their own invention.

When writing imaginatively, children are freed from the task of having to remember real events. They are in charge of characters and action, and can manipulate and order events. There is also a possibility that through the making and modelling of imagined characters and worlds, the child can actually make sense of his or her own experience.

The varied action and multiple events that occur in story writing can result in long, sustained pieces of work. Although quantity of writing must never be mistaken for quality, children gain great satisfaction from occasionally producing a lengthy, sustained piece of writing.

BACKGROUND

How easy is it?

The short answer is that it isn't easy at all. However, children are often more motivated to write stories than anything else, because they can see more point to story-writing. They have listened to a great many stories. They know the form a story takes and understand that others want to hear them. The idea of writing stories that others will read makes sense.

This is an important point. It is imperative that children's stories are read and enjoyed by others. Unless this happens, the whole reason for story-writing is lost. A tick at the end, or a smiling sticker, is a poor reward for efforts which have been deprived of real readers and therefore real purpose.

Story-writers need support

Writing should not be a frustrating and lonely experience. If there are children in your class who stare despairingly at their blank paper during story-writing sessions, they probably require a more structured and supportive environment for imaginative writing. Children often need to talk about particular parts of their story, but the overworked teacher can't be in two places at once.

For this reason, it is a good idea to provide a context for writing and to encourage story-writing groups where children work together.

How can a context help?

This chapter describes how to use teacher-created contexts in order to develop a supportive, contextual approach to imaginative story-writing.

Children operate well in the world of imagination and are motivated by the conventions of story-writing, but they often imagine a great deal more than they could ever write into their story. Knowing that the story will not be able to hold too much detail, they fail to, or are unable to, think the details through. Discussion helps to set the scene and encourages children to delineate their invented places clearly and to draw their characters carefully; in essence, to think the story through in greater detail. A particular context may last just one lesson, or could be spread over several sessions encouraging longer, sustained pieces of work.

What will the children learn?

Through writing within a context, children learn to question inconsistencies, and to spot when a series of events is unclear or a character badly delineated. They learn to modify their own writing in the light of this informed criticism. Reading aloud, editing, drafting and redrafting are used to help achieve the best results. Finally, they learn that at the heart of all writing lies the necessity to consider how the reader will respond, and to bear in mind what the reader needs to know.

ACTIVITIES

1. Strange creatures

Age range
Five to seven.

Group size
Individuals and the whole class.

What you need
Large, black footprints (human or animal-shaped), writing and drawing materials, photocopiable sheet 172 (for further activity only).

What to do
Before the children arrive at school, cut out as many large, black footprints as possible and use them to make a trail on the walls, windows and ceiling of the classroom. The trail should have a definite entry and exit point, perhaps a window or a door. When the children arrive, wait until they notice the trail and then encourage them to speculate about the sort of animal or being that might have made it, where it entered and left the room and why it chose their classroom.

Ask the children to draw or paint the sort of creature that might leave such prints. They should then write a short piece about why the creature came into the classroom and why it had to leave before they arrived in the morning.

The children's work should be shared and displayed beside the trail.

Further activity
Encourage the class to invent longer stories about their creatures and act them out during drama lessons. These stories could then be written down, either by the children themselves using photocopiable page 172, or with an older child or adult acting as a scribe.

2. Oh no!

Age range
Five to seven.

Group size
Individuals.

What you need
Writing materials.

What to do
This activity can be completed over several sessions. Tell the class that they are each going to write a story, which will be told in words and pictures. (They will have seen plenty of good story-books which do this.) Give each of the children a piece of paper, with the words 'One day I went out...' written at the bottom either by you or by the children themselves. The children must decide where they went and what they were doing, and draw a picture to show this; it might be going out to play, shopping, taking the dog for a walk, visiting a relative, going swimming, going to the circus or anything else they choose.

Then ask them to think of something that could go wrong, either on the way or when they arrive at their destination. Give each child a new sheet of paper with the words 'Oh no!' written at the bottom. Ask them to draw the disaster. You may choose to encourage them to expand on their drawing by adding some writing of their own.

At this point, you may ask some children to share their

Its feet are drity and it hates the wet. It came to see our hamster

situations and disasters with the rest of the class. Emphasise the diversity of the situations and problems, and build up excitement about what is going to happen next.

Give each child another sheet with the words 'Oh no!' written at the bottom. Ask them to think of another mishap that could occur, and to draw and write about this. Finally, give them a blank sheet with nothing written on it. On this, they should show how the story ends and whether the problems are resolved or not. They can decide themselves what should be written at the bottom of this sheet.

Once the stories have been completed, they should be mounted and made into individual story books. These should be read to the class and to groups of children by both the teacher and the children themselves.

3. The outing

Age range
Five to seven.

Group size
Individuals, small groups or the whole class.

What you need
Mr Gumpy's Outing by John Burningham (Cape/Puffin), writing materials.

What to do
Read *Mr Gumpy's Outing* to the class. Ask the children to imagine that, like Mr Gumpy, they are going on a river trip. Which people or animals do they think they might ask to come with them, and what stipulations would they make

before letting these passengers on to the boat?

You might choose to organise this so that each child in the class or group suggests a character, combining these to form one group story. Alternatively, you could ask each child to write and illustrate his or her own story. Obviously, a group story is most effective when it is about people with whom the whole group is familiar; the school crossing lady, the cook, the caretaker, children in the class or favourite teachers (' "Can I come too?" asked Miss Dale. "All right, but don't play that piano" ').

4. My secret friend

Age range
Six to eight.

Group size
Individuals or pairs.

What you need
Writing materials.

What to do
Ask the children to invent an imaginary friend who helps them. Tell them that the friend can be human or non-human.

Her name would be Jane. I'd want her just to be my friend really.

Ask the children each to draw a picture of their secret friend, and to write about a time when they would have liked to have had such a friend to help them, what help they wanted and what they might have done if they had received the help.

5. Father Christmas at home

Age range
Six to eight.

Group size
Individuals, pairs and the whole class.

What you need
Photocopiable page 173, writing materials.

What to do
Ask the class what they imagine Father Christmas to look like. Suggest that the clothes and accoutrements they mention are only the things he uses for work. But where do they think he lives, what does his house look like and what does he do in his leisure time?

Split the class into pairs and ask them to discuss what they think are Father Christmas's favourite food, television programme, non-work clothes and hobbies. Ask them to imagine his parents. What do he and his friends like doing when not at work? Who *are* his friends? Does he have a best friend? Do the children think he is married?

While the children are doing this, listen to what they are saying in their pairs, but do not invite anyone to share their ideas with the class, since this might inhibit others' ideas.

Show the class photocopiable page 173 and explain how to use it as a springboard for writing. Each child should fill in the details required and write a few short sentences to elaborate on their drawings or the reasons for

their choices. Then ask the children to write about what Father Christmas might do at home when he is not working.

6. A place to play

Age range
Seven to nine.

Group size
Pairs, groups of three and the whole class.

What you need
A collection of sticks, stones, grass, Plasticine and other modelling materials, adhesive, sticky tape, writing materials.

What to do
Talk to the children about the times when they have created a secret camp with a group of friends. Tell them to use the modelling materials provided to create a model camp in their groups of two or three.

Each group should decide:
• what sort of area the camp is in;
• who created it;
• why it was built;
• whether there are any rules for the camp;
• whether there is a secret password.

The writing session could begin with each child inventing and writing about one character who helped create the camp. Then give each group a limited amount of time, say 15 minutes, to read and discuss the character descriptions and to produce a few lines which answer the above questions.

Each child should then write his or her own, separate story about an incident that took place at the camp. You can choose how you want to do

this. The children could decide, individually or as a group, what each incident was and which member of the group is to write it up. Alternatively, you could give each child a card with the title of an incident, such as 'A stranger arrives', 'An argument develops', 'Danger at the camp' or 'The camp is discovered'.

Once all the children in the group have written a first draft of their story, they should read it to the others, asking for suggestions and ideas for improvement. Completed stories should be made into a book and displayed beside the model. The children should be encouraged to read the other stories about their camp, and also the work of other groups.

7. A journey into fantasy

Age range
Seven to nine.

Group size
Individuals and pairs.

What you need
Writing materials, cards with statements written on them (see below).

What to do
Young children are well known for their tireless ability to follow their parents' most mundane and apparently indisputable explanations with the question 'Why?'. Children aged from seven to nine will readily identify this technique and delight in the way it can quickly drive even the most patient adult insane.

Begin with the whole class. Select a volunteer and ask her

to choose an initial statement from a number that you have prepared. All the statements should be fairly mundane; 'I'm just going out', 'I'm going to see your teacher', 'I'm feeling really tired' and so on.

The volunteer reads out the statement, and you ask 'Why?'. She must then answer with a short explanation, which may be as down-to-earth or as wild and unlikely as she pleases. Whatever she says, you again ask 'Why?'. The game continues for as long as possible.

Once they understand what is required, divide the children into pairs and give them an opportunity to play the game themselves. Ask some pairs to 'replay' their conversation for the class at the end.

Then ask each child to choose an initial statement and write a conversation along the same lines. The children may choose to use ideas from their work in pairs, or to make up their own responses.

The finished writing should be shared, discussed and displayed for others to read.

8. Story in a bag

Age range
Seven to ten.

Group size
Pairs, groups of six to eight and the whole class.

What you need
Large sack containing both unusual and everyday items, writing materials.

What to do
Children need plenty of confidence for this activity, and they quickly improve with practice. It is therefore wise to begin by asking the children simply to invent the story and tell it orally, only moving to a written response when confidence and fluency have been achieved.

Tell the class that there are several important, unusual and interesting items in the big sack. Each item has a story behind it. Begin the session by inviting one of the children to dip into the sack and pick out an object. Whatever they find, you will invent and tell a story about it.

Then tell the class that it is their turn to become story-tellers. Ask each pair of children to select an object from the sack. They must decide to whom the object belongs and why it is special, and invent a story about something that has happened to it in the past. Allow the children some time to discuss these questions and to invent their story.

Split the class into groups of about six or eight children. Discuss how a story begins and ends and how the story-teller uses voice, mannerisms and techniques such as repetition and exclamation to maintain interest.

Each pair in the group must decide whether they will share the story-telling or, if not, which of them will tell the story. They then have three minutes to tell a story to the rest of the group.

Following this session, the children should feel much more confident about writing their stories. Children should be encouraged to work together on the stories in pairs.

They could do this in several ways. For example, both children could write different parts of the story, or they could simply discuss the different ways of beginning the story and compose it together, taking it in turns to act as scribe. Either way, rough drafts of the story should be read to the larger group, who should be encouraged to ask questions and offer comment and positive criticism.

Final copies of the stories should be decorated and displayed in the form of a class book, which could be used for story-telling sessions with younger classes.

Further activity
If the children have enjoyed this activity, they may like to try it again. This time, allow them to create their own

agenda by each bringing one object from home. Then put the children into groups of three. They must create a story which incorporates all three objects brought in by the group members.

9. The key

Age range
Seven to ten.

Group size
Pairs and individuals.

What you need
Photocopiable page 174, writing materials.

What to do
You may need two sessions for this activity.

Tell the children that they are going to write a story about a strange and unusual key. Give each pair a copy of photocopiable page 174, and tell them to read the questions carefully and to jot down as many different answers to each question as they can. The answers should be as wild and diverse as possible, encouraging the children to think laterally about all the possibilities of a story before deciding on one particular line of thought.

Next, ask the pairs of children to choose the question that they think is the most important. This may be because it has the most exciting answer or because they see it as a fundamental question, without which any story about the key would be meaningless.

Having decided on this, they should choose one of the possible answers to the question. If they don't like any of these, they can invent

another answer to use. This will then form the basis of the story. The children should decide which other questions will be important for their story, and which answers they will use, marking these with a small cross. As before, if they find that none of the answers is appropriate, they should invent another. The children should then invent the linking parts of the story, and together write the 'bare-bones' structure which will form the first draft.

It is often productive to end the first session at this stage. The children should certainly be allowed a break before they start to flesh the story out.

Begin the next session by getting the children to read their 'bare-bones' structure. Explain that the rest of the work will be done individually, but that they may consult in their pairs if they need another opinion, or some help.

The children should systematically elaborate each section of their structures. They could start by deciding on an original, attention-grabbing way to begin the story, and developing it to maintain a high level of descriptive detail and action. Emphasise that you expect the members of each pair to produce stories that are quite different.

10. Creating mood in a story

Age range
Eight to twelve.

Group size
Individuals and pairs.

What you need
Atmospheric pictures or photographs, paper.

What to do
Give out one picture to each pair, with one piece of paper for each child and one joint piece of paper per pair. Allow one minute's silence for the children to study their pictures carefully. Using the joint paper, ask the children to brainstorm all the words which could describe the mood of the picture. Then each child can choose the one word which best sums up the mood. Each child should write his chosen word at the top of his own sheet of paper. Explain that all the writing which follows must try to capture this mood.

The children must do the rest of the writing on their own. Each child must decide

which five things about the picture help to capture this mood, and list them down the centre of their page. Taking each listed aspect of the picture in turn, they should think of two words to describe it, and then write these in front of the word they describe to produce a short phrase. Next the children should look at their picture and note any smells or sounds of which they would be aware if they were in the picture. These ideas should be used to produce a short descriptive paragraph which captures the mood of the picture.

Ask the children to imagine that they are standing just out of view of the camera. They should write a few sentences to describe how they feel as they look at the scene ahead. Finally, they should think of something which could have happened immediately before the photograph was taken which reinforces the mood and feelings they have been describing.

The children should work on these lines until the description of the experience or event is as concise as possible. Then they can add it to the main body of writing as the final explanation for the mood of the photograph.

Mount the children's work and display each piece beside the photograph to which it refers. Children should be encouraged to read all the work and each to find a piece which prompts them to ask questions about the story behind the final sentence. These can be written into a special 'Comments' book or displayed beside each piece, or alternatively they could be shared when the writing is read to the class.

11. Fairytale introductions

Age range
Eight to twelve.

Group size
Pairs.

What you need
List of fairytale characters, writing materials.

What to do
Ask the whole class to think of as many fairytale characters as possible, listing the names on a large piece of paper. Then ask the children to form pairs. Each child in the pair should choose one character whom he feels he knows quite well, making sure that no pair has two characters from the same story.

Tell the pairs to discuss between them what might happen if one of their characters 'got lost' and ended up in their partner's story by mistake. They should decide:
• which of the two fairytale settings offers the most potential for this type of story;
• when in the fairytale the 'lost' character appears;
• what happens.

The children could write the story individually or together. They might decide to write it as a straight tale, saying how the chosen fairytale is altered by the sudden appearance of the displaced character. Alternatively, one child might write the story in this way, while the other tells the tale from the viewpoint of the displaced character, saying how he or she came to be displaced and describing his or her first experience in the new situation.

The finished stories should be illustrated, written up in best fairytale style and made into a book. Titles could take the form of an introduction: 'Red Riding Hood meets Rapunzel' or 'The Wicked Wolf meets the Witch'. The authors should be encouraged to read their stories to groups of younger children in the school.

12. Wild stories

Age range
Eight to twelve.

Group size
Individuals or pairs.

What you need
Writing materials.

What to do
Introduce the class to the game of 'wild stories'. In pairs, the children should finish the sentence 'Sorry I'm late, but...'. Each partner must take it in turns to think of an excuse which is wilder and more fantastic than the last. Invite a couple of volunteers to share their wild excuses with the rest of the class.

Then tell the children that they are going to do a similar thing, but this time as individuals, and based around the phrase 'It wasn't me...'. Each child should think of three to six progressively more improbable stories about how and why the window/vase/chair/ornament came to be broken (or whatever situation you choose to attach to the phrase).

The completed pieces of work should be illustrated and made into a book to be displayed in the classroom for others to read.

13. Unknown characters

Age range
Eight to twelve.

Group size
Individuals and pairs.

What you need
Magazines, scissors, writing materials, photocopiable page 175.

What to do
Give out the magazines, and ask the children to see whether they can find and cut out a picture of someone who looks very different from themselves.

Tell them to look closely at this picture and think about the person. They should then invent a name, job, hobbies, personality and family background for this person. Photocopiable page 175 may be used to help create this mini-biography.

Then ask the children to choose one of the following options:
• Write a story about a visit or outing for the person in their picture, deciding where she went and why, how she felt about going and what happened during the visit and afterwards.

• Write a story about an argument the person was involved in, describing who the argument was with, why it started and how their chosen individual felt about it, both privately and in public.

Further activity
The children could form working pairs, each reading their imaginary biography and story to their partner, who should comment constructively and ask as many questions as necessary about the personality and background of the imaginary character.

The pairs can then invent a story about what happens when their two characters meet. Before they start working, emphasise that the children must take an equal responsibility for composing and writing the story. Once finished, the biographies and stories should be mounted and displayed beside the photographs. The children could also be asked to comment on how well they feel they worked together, and to discuss where difficulties arose and how these were resolved.

14. Story types: the complete storybook

Age range
Nine to twelve.

Group size
Individuals.

What you need
Writing materials.

What to do
This activity will probably take two sessions.

First session
Begin by talking to the children about the different types of story they enjoy reading. Get the whole class to brainstorm as many different types of children's story as possible.

In pairs, ask the children to think of one particularly good example of each type of story and to write a definition which says how that type differs from the others. Discuss and collate these definitions.

Having discussed the story types, suggest that the class begins to create a 'complete storybook'. This should contain as many different types of story as possible. Emphasise that the book will be created by the whole class, over a long period of time (perhaps half a term), and will draw on writing done at home as well as at school. It will be up to individuals to suggest that their work be included in the book. No one will be coerced into submitting stories.

Second session
Ask individuals to decide on a particular type of story that they would like to try writing. Tell them that they will not be asked to write the whole story, but should decide on a title and write an opening paragraph which indicates what sort of story it will be. Some children will be very keen to finish their story, having waited for a long time to be given this freedom in their writing lessons. Others will be less eager. All the children should produce a title and a really good opening paragraph, but those who do not wish to continue beyond this point should not be made to do so.

Children should be encouraged to read each other's work and to guess what type of story the author was writing. All titles and opening paragraphs should be displayed in the classroom under headings which indicate the type of story that the author was aiming for. Obviously, any child who finishes a whole story and is particularly pleased with it can ask for his work to be included in the relevant section of the 'Complete storybook'.

15. Strange postures

Age range
Nine to twelve.

Group size
Groups of five to six.

What you need
Magazine photographs of groups of people, space for drama, writing materials.

What to do
Divide the class into groups of five to six children. Each group should elect an 'arranger', who will not participate in the action. Give each arranger a photograph from a magazine. He or she must study it carefully, and then arrange the members of the group into positions similar to those of the people in the photograph. No other member of the group is allowed to see the photograph, and the arranger is not allowed to inform the group members about the photograph's background details or context.

Once the group members are all in position, the arranger calls 'action', and the group must improvise a story, assuming characters, relationships and actions that are suggested by their positions. This is often very good fun, and allows the children to establish strong characters and contexts.

When the improvised scene is over, all the children in the group should be asked to write either a prelude or a sequel to the scenario they have just acted out. The children should do this independently, and still without looking at the original photograph. Once finished, they should read their work to others in the group and decide whether they would like to present it in the form of a class book of short stories.

Finally, if the children wish, they may see the original photograph from which the positions were derived – it will be nothing like their stories!

16. Private thoughts, actual dialogue

Age range
Nine to twelve.

Group size
Individuals and pairs.

What you need
Photocopiable page 176, writing materials, chalkboard.

What to do
Give out one drawing from photocopiable page 176 to each pair of children. Allow the children one minute to study the picture carefully. Each partner must decide which character he or she will adopt and then, writing from that character's point of view, must produce an individual piece of writing to explain:
• how the character feels about what has just happened;

• how the character feels about the other person;
• how the character came to be in this situation;
• what the character would like to say or do to the other, but can't;
• why the character can't say or do it.

Now the pair must decide which character speaks first. The child who has written about that character must think of something the character might say, and write this down. The other partner then writes the response on the next line. This should continue until the conversation is completed.

Finally, each child should write about what happens after this conversation and how his or her character feels about it.

The writing about the characters' own feelings should be mounted and displayed beneath the picture and the conversation.

17. School history

Age range
Nine to twelve.

Group size
Groups of four.

What you need
Old school record books, writing materials, space for drama if required.

What to do
Many schools keep the headteacher's day record book, which often goes back many years. Such books record the day-to-day events of the school, visitors to the school, punishments meted out to particular children, and so on.

They provide a valuable record of what schools were like in the past, and can be a very real way to bring history alive.

If your school has such a record book, show it to the class. From the evidence in its pages, encourage the children to imagine what it was like to be a pupil or a teacher years ago. Ask each group to choose one event and try to reconstruct what happened. This can be done in a drama lesson, or through group discussion.

In order to make the story realistic, children will have to invent details and characters, possibly using the book as a source for names and details about the school routine.

Children should then work in pairs to write their reconstructed story from the point of view of one of the characters involved. Once finished, these stories should be displayed beside a photocopy of the relevant page from the original day record book.

18. The party

Age range
Nine to twelve.

Group size
Individuals.

What you need
Writing and drawing equipment.

What to do
Ask the children to draw a picture of the best party they can imagine. Then tell them to describe the atmosphere of that party, thinking about:
• the sounds;
• the movement;

• how they feel in their party clothes;
• the expression on the faces of others;
• the temperature outside and inside the party;
• what is happening in the different areas of the party;
• the feelings they have about the other people and the situation.

Only the title should mention what the party is for and why they are there.

19. Inner thoughts

Age range
Ten to twelve.

Group size
Individuals.

What you need
Suitable music or abstract picture, writing materials.

What to do
Select an evocative piece of music or abstract picture. It is probably easiest to use music the first time you try this activity.

Choose a time when the children are in a quiet, responsive mood, and make sure that each member of the class has a piece of paper and a pencil to hand.

Before introducing the music or picture, explain that the intention of a composer or artist is always to produce a piece of work which provokes a response or feeling in the audience. The audience in its turn has to be receptive and to give free rein to the imagination. Individual responses may be broadly similar but, because they necessarily depend on

imagination and personal experiences, no two will be exactly the same.

Describe the sort of atmosphere that is necessary to allow imagination and private thoughts to flourish. The mood should be quiet and reflective; closed eyes may help to prevent distractions. In the case of music, images may also help focus the imagination; a flickering flame, mist or cloud which slowly envelops and banishes irrelevant concerns, helping children to concentrate and allow their minds to become like a blank screen upon which the imagination can work freely.

Once you feel that the class is receptive, introduce the chosen music or picture quietly and without any

warning. Allow a suitable length of time for the children to reflect silently. Then, speaking very quietly, ask them to write down single words or phrases which reflect their thoughts. They should write as many as possible, not worrying about spelling at this stage, or trying to write complete sentences. This should be done very quietly.

Then ask the children to write in detail about the strongest image or images that came to them, and to describe these in a way that reflects how they felt. They will probably use many of the words and phrases that they have already written. Final copies of the work should be shared with one friend in the class, but displayed only if the author so chooses.

CHAPTER 5

Imaginative writing in a context

This chapter describes how children can work as a group to create a context for writing. The contexts provided in this chapter are divided into sections for the age ranges five to seven, seven to nine and nine to twelve. The contexts are developed through a series of tasks, both individual and collaborative, whereby children gradually invent the places and characters featured in their stories.

When children build their own contexts for writing, they become the experts on the setting, history and characters. As its creators, they know far more about it than their teacher. When individual members of a group write stories set within the same context, they are prepared and able to give each other specific, high-quality, informed advice, as well as support and inspiration. The feedback is direct, from one creator to another, one writer to another, bound together by their shared understanding of the context.

Working this way develops collaborative attitudes as well as vital writing skills. The contexts suggested for junior-aged children each culminate in an extended story written by the group. Through writing together children learn that in the face of challenge, writers have to think about the small details of their writing. They learn to question when the action is unclear and to temper criticism with analysis. When producing a chapter for the final story, each writer will have reflected upon previous comments, and may modify his or her work as a result.

Ourselves

Each of the following activities for five- to seven-year-olds may require several separate sessions. It is for you to judge how long the sessions should be and how many are required.

1. Creating the street

Age range
Five to seven.

Group size
Groups of about six.

What you need
Shoe boxes or similar, card, craft materials, writing materials, scissors, adhesive, magazines.

What to do
First of all, the group must create the street which will star in their story. The children could use grey, black and brown paper to represent the road and pavements. They should discuss what road markings might be seen, and paint these on to the road. While someone does this, the other children could pencil in the pavement slabs. Explain that this is a residential street, and the houses have not yet been made. As children finish work on the road and pavement, ask them to look through the magazines and find pictures of people who might live in this street. These pictures should be cut out and mounted on card, leaving a tab at the bottom which can be folded under in order to make each character stand up.

Once enough characters have been cut out and mounted on card, ask the children to decide which of these people live together and which live alone. Begin by asking each member of the group to suggest a possible household. This is a good opportunity for the children to consider and discuss different types of household groups. The children should be encouraged to justify their choices and discuss alternatives before making a final decision.

Once they have split the characters into family groups and households, each child or pair of children should take responsibility for one household. Ask them to choose names for the characters, and write these on the back. If they haven't already done so, they should decide how the people are related to each other and what they do for a living.

Each family will need a house or a flat in which to live. Allow the children to choose a suitable box and to make a house or flat for their family. These should then be placed along the street.

The children can then write and draw about the people who live in the house they have made. Ask each child to share his or her work with the group before it is mounted and displayed in the classroom.

Encourage the children to play freely with their characters and the street. Since six children may be too large a group to do this at one time, allocate separate play sessions with three or four children in each.

2. A story about the street

Age range
Five to seven.

Group size
Groups of about six.

What you need
The model street (see Activity 1, page 68), writing materials for display, chalkboard or easel.

What to do
The children can begin to invent a story about their street and the people who live in it. There are two ways in which you can help them to do this.

The first approach is to give the group a series of happenings and ask them to use the characters to play out a story. You might, for example, say 'Someone has a birthday', 'Someone gets lost' or 'Someone gets into trouble'. The children must then decide which character is to be the focus of the incident, and what happens. However, some young children find it very hard to invent a story that has not arisen from their own train of thought. As a result, they may produce a story-line which seems disjointed, uninspired and lacking in originality, or which has been too much influenced by your suggestions and so has not been truly created by the children themselves.

Another approach, which avoids this problem, is simply to ask the children 'What do you think could happen in this street?' and see what they suggest. If they have had plenty of opportunity to play freely with the characters and the model of the street, they will probably have lots of ideas.

In this situation, you should encourage the children to tell a clear, consistent story. Any questions you ask should be to clarify your understanding of the story, or to encourage the children to clarify their own meaning, whether to themselves or to each other. You should be particularly wary of 'interpreting' the story for the children or of providing too many specific ideas of your own. Instead of providing direct suggestions, it may be better to pose questions which encourage the children to generate alternatives which can then be discussed.

When the children have agreed on a story, ask the whole group to sit in front of a large piece of display paper pinned to an easel. Explain that you are going to write their story down so that it can be told to the rest of the class. Make it clear that the whole group is going to tell you what to write.

Ask the children for suggestions about how the story could begin, and discuss their various ideas until all the group members agree on the best way.

Throughout this story-writing process, your role as teacher will be to raise the children's awareness of the language of story-telling. One of your aims will be to help them to develop an 'ear' for written language and how it differs from speech. You can do this by frequently rereading what the group has written so far, and by suggesting (or encouraging the children to suggest) alternative ways to phrase things. It is important to ask the children themselves to decide which of the possible alternatives is the most effective.

3. Illustrating the story

Age range
Five to seven.

Group size
Groups of about six.

What you need
Writing and drawing equipment.

What to do
Once you have written out the whole story (see Activity 2), read it back to the group. Explain that you are going to copy their story out on to small pieces of paper and bind the sheets together to make a book.

Ask the children how they think the story should be divided, which parts should have pictures and why. Try to find as many sections requiring pictures as there are children in the group, and ask each child to take responsibility for drawing one picture.

When they have done this, either you or the children can copy the story into suitable sections, mount the illustrations and the writing and bind the pages together to make a book (see Chapter 10). If you wish, the children's original work describing the characters can also be added. The children should be given an opportunity to hear their story read to the rest of the class. Encourage them to tell the others how the story was created.

Holidays

Before beginning these activities, you may like to read the class some extracts from *The Hobbit* by J.R.R. Tolkien. Discuss the immensely detailed land and characters that Tolkien had to invent before writing his epic story. The activities in this chapter will involve the children, too, in creating a land and the creatures who inhabit it, and the readings from *The Hobbit* will indicate the potential for magic within the story.

1. Inventing an island

Age range
Seven to nine.

Group size
Five or six children, who must work in the same group for all tasks in this section.

What you need
Photocopiable page 177, writing and drawing materials.

What to do
Tell the children that each group is going to write an epic adventure story set on a remote island in the middle of the ocean. Before beginning the story, they must first create the land and the characters who populate it. Give one copy of photocopiable page 177 to each group. Discuss the map with the children, noting the names of the various locations and the images these conjure up. Explain that at the moment the island is uninhabited.

First, the group must assign each member to a different location on the map. Each child must take responsibility for inventing the detail of his or her area, drawing a picture of the location and marking on any buildings, structures or landmarks which might be there. The pictures must be as detailed as possible.

As they draw, the children should be thinking about how they will describe this place to the rest of the group. Once finished, they should show and describe their area to the others, who should ask questions to clarify the description. The children *must* understand that it is essential to listen to each person in the group, so that everyone becomes familiar with the terrain.

This may be the first time that the children have been encouraged to question each other in this way, and they may need some help in recognising when important details are missing and in learning how to show appreciation for each other's work. This sort of questioning is an essential skill. Opportunities must be taken to teach it to the children and to allow them to practise it.

Finally, ask the children to write about the location they have drawn. The writing can be displayed beside a copy of the map. Each group in the class should be given the opportunity to look at the other groups' islands and to read the descriptions, comparing them with their own. This is fun, and helps ensure an interested audience for the written work.

Further activity
One child from each group can give a brief conducted tour of the island to another group.

2. Populating the land

Age range
Seven to nine.

Group size
Groups of five or six.

What you need
Interesting mix of collage materials (shiny ones are particularly good), access to the display of maps and places.

What to do
The children will probably need several sessions to complete this activity. Explain to them that they each have to invent and write about something or someone who lives in one of the places drawn on their group's map. They must understand that this is a magic land, and the characters do not have to be human; they may take any shape or form the children wish. The only stipulation is that the character they invent must live in a place drawn by someone else in the group.

BLACK BLOOD MOON

In black blood moon lots of horrible things happen. Shades is the one who lives there. There are bats rats and dead cats. The only noises you can hear are screams and shouts. Its a horrible place.

The first thing for the group to decide is who will create a character for each place. This will probably involve a certain amount of debate, which gives an opportunity for the children to practise their collaborative skills.

The children can then create the characters using collage techniques. Although the characters are totally imaginary, the children must take account of where they live and consider such ideas as:
• what and how they eat;
• when and where they sleep;
• how they communicate;
• how they move;
• what they are called;
• which other characters are the creatures friends or enemies.

When the craft work is finished, ask the children to describe their characters to each other, exploring relationships. This gives an opportunity for children to firm up their ideas and to iron out any inconsistencies before writing.

Ask the children to write a biography for their character, which will be read to their group. You may need to discuss this with the class and list the sort of information that should be included.

The group must listen to each first draft and ask questions about important details that are missing, point out inconsistencies, and so on. This is another opportunity to practise the skills introduced in Activity 1 (page 70). It is also an introduction to the idea of drafting written work, and can be used to demonstrate both how and why drafting is done. Changes should be indicated using arrows, lines or asterisks to indicate where additions or alterations should go. You can either introduce a uniform system for this or allow the children to devise their own.

Once the children have inserted their additions, they *must* read their writing from start to finish, only copying it out when they are satisfied with it. Some children may need a break before copying out their work and mounting it on paper. If possible, this should be allowed. Specially sharpened (new?) pencils and crisp, clean paper can add a special air of celebration to this final process.

Finally, all characters and writing should be added to the display beside the appropriate location. Once again, children will enjoy sharing their work and seeing that of other groups.

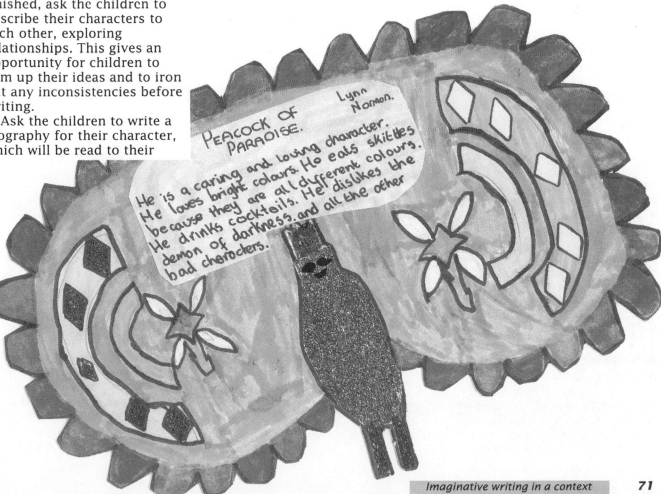

PEACOCK OF PARADISE.   Lynn Norman.

He is a caring and loving character. He loves bright colours. He eats skittles because they are all different colours. He drinks cocktails. He dislikes the demon of darkness, and all the other bad characters.

3. Impressions of the island: writing a play

Age range
Seven to nine.

Group size
Groups of about five or six.

What you need
Writing materials.

What to do
By doing the previous two activities (see pages 70 and 71) the children will have built up a comprehensive picture of life on the island. Having created the land, they need to retreat from it a little. Therefore, leave a short time, perhaps a few days, before starting this activity.

Explain that a grand adventure is about to unfold. The children must forget that they have created this island and imagine that they are seeing it for the very first time.

Tell each group that they have won a holiday to Disneyland and are on their way when their plane develops a mechanical fault and they are forced to land on a small island. As they stumble out of the plane, ask them to describe what they see and decide how to explore the island. What sort of things do they say to each other as they look around? What do they see, smell and hear? How do they feel? Tell the children that they have 15 minutes to perfect a *very* short drama that will be acted out in front of the rest of the class.

It is important to recognise that in this drama exercise, the group are building an imaginative dialogue, supported by a well-known context. After each group's performance, be encouraging and point out the successful ideas that emerge. Ask for comments from the audience. Emphasise that critical comments will only be allowed if they are positive and show a way forward; destructive criticism will not be tolerated.

Through acting out the play, the children will have the script firmly established in their heads. They can now write their play, concentrating on the conventions of script-writing.

Explain that nothing is written in a script but the words spoken by the actors, together with a few necessary stage directions. The names of the characters are printed at the side of the page and a new line is begun each time someone new speaks. They may like to just print the initials of each character to save time. Each piece of dialogue should begin with a capital letter, but there is no need to use speech marks since everything that is written must be spoken – apart from the stage directions which will be written in parentheses.

Further activity
Later on in the project, these plays could be shown to a younger class as a preview of the epic novel that will be produced.

4. The evil winged character

Age range
Seven to nine.

Group size
Groups of five or six.

What you need
Collage materials, writing materials, points listed on chalkboard.

What to do
Remind the children about the plays they have written in Activity 3. Tell them that as they stand in this strange land, suddenly everything is plunged into darkness as the huge wings of an evil creature block out the sunlight. The winged creature hovers in the air, screeching out a terrible message.

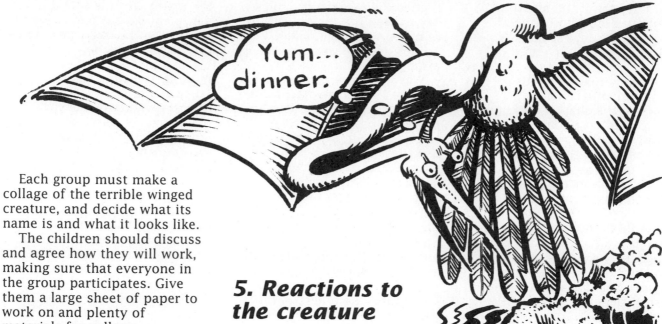

Each group must make a collage of the terrible winged creature, and decide what its name is and what it looks like.

The children should discuss and agree how they will work, making sure that everyone in the group participates. Give them a large sheet of paper to work on and plenty of materials for collage.

The groups will become familiar with the creature as they create it, and when it is completed you can ask each group to make decisions about the following points, with a scribe to record what has been decided.

• Where has the creature come from?
• What are its intentions?
• What is it saying as it calls out across the land?
• What are the immediate reactions of the local inhabitants?
• What does their group, stranded on the island, do?

Pin each group's creature above their display with a speech bubble coming from its mouth to show what it is saying. The name of the creature and the writing on its background and purpose should be displayed beside it.

Further activity
Children may enjoy writing a detailed, evocative description of the evil creature. These could be written as poems.

5. Reactions to the creature

Age range
Seven to nine.

Group size
Groups of five or six.

What you need
Drawing and writing materials, felt-tipped pens, card.

What to do
Remind the children that different characters will react differently to the sudden arrival of this creature. Ask them to draw the face of the collage character they invented for Activity 2. In a bubble above this character, they should write what it is thinking as it sees and hears the creature. Each child must then draw her own face with another thought bubble containing her own thoughts on seeing the creature.

These should be added to the display below the creature, showing the many different points of view about the same scene.

6. Writing an epic adventure

Age range
Seven to nine.

Group size
Groups of five or six.

What you need
Writing materials, photocopiable pages 177 and 178.

What to do
Explain to the groups that together they are going to write an epic adventure story about the island they have created and the battle with the evil winged creature. Each child will write a chapter, one after the other, and the battle will only be resolved in the final chapter.

Choose an author for Chapter 1, which will describe the first part of the story, and remind him of the opening sentences on photocopiable page 177. He must include himself and his invented character in the action and the story must end at a cliff-hanging point.

When the chapter has been completed it should be read to the rest of the group, and a volunteer can then be chosen to write Chapter 2.

Each chapter must begin with the last sentence of the previous chapter, thus providing both continuity and a beginning for the new writer. When a rough draft has been written for each chapter, the writer should read this to the rest of the group who will 'troubleshoot' it, looking for inconsistency of character, place or storyline.

Once a chapter has been altered and finally accepted by the group, the writer can copy it out for presentation, placing photocopiable page 178 under a blank sheet of paper to provide guidelines.

Once the first rough chapter has been written, remind the children how to question and criticise constructively, and clarify any additional information and rules.

For example, we suggest that:
• characters can only be 'wiped out' or killed by their creator;
• when writing a chapter, the writer must include himself and his character as well as anybody else or any other character that fits the storyline;
• the writer mustn't tell *anybody* what he is writing until he has finished his chapter, unless he is really stuck, in which case he can ask for a little help.

You may find that you have to keep stopping the class to remind them about the rules. Try to keep the tone of these reminders positive, using groups that are working well as examples.

When the first child comes to copy out his chapter, make some suggestions about presentation to the whole class; for example, they could use a big, decorated initial letter at the start of the chapter as in old-fashioned story-books. Stress the importance of careful, clear handwriting and so on. (See Chapter 10 on presentation and display for other ideas and teaching points.)

While each child is writing his chapter the others in the group should be getting on with tasks from the following list. You may find it necessary to organise a 'tick list' for each group so that they can keep track of who is doing what. It is also a good idea to have a rule that all work be shown to the other group members before it is stuck on to anyone else's work.

Decorating borders
Finished writing will be mounted on a larger sheet of card, leaving space for a border around the edge. This can be decorated like an illuminated manuscript to make the story-book attractive and special. Each child will decorate his or her own borders, and this can be done before or after the finished work is mounted.

Making the book
See Chapter 10 on presentation and display for ideas on how to do this.

Writing the book title
Once the group has decided what the story is to be called, the writing for the title can be designed and cut out, ready to stick on to the front cover once this has been made.

Making the title page
This should include the book title, the names of the authors, the name of a publisher, real or imaginary, the publisher's logo, the date and place of publication, and so on.

Contents page
This will need to have a decorated border and a heading, ready for the chapter headings to be added as they are completed.

Mini-biography of the writers
A small photo and a few lines about each of the writers will be required for the back of the book.

Summary or introduction to the book
The group may wish to include a summary of the story, or a brief description of how the book came to be written.

Letters to other teachers and classes
These should explain about the book, giving an approximate date when it is due to be finished and asking if any of the other classes in the school would be interested to see and read it.

Posters to advertise the book
The children will probably come up with plenty of ideas for poster designs.

The ideas are endless, but if you run out of activities, which seems unlikely, you could allow the children to organise a book-launch. However, maybe that is another project!

Schools

At the start of this project, aimed at nine- to twelve-year-olds, suggest to the children that copies of the work produced by the class be sent to a children's television channel, along with a covering letter which explains the project and asks for comments on the likelihood of really having the series made. Chapter 2 gives advice about how to teach the children to write such a letter.

It is extremely important that at the end of this project the children read the work of other groups in the class and note the diversity which has arisen in spite of the same starting points.

It may help you first to read the advice contained in Activities 1 and 6 on pages 70 and 73.

1. Creating the characters

Age range
Nine to twelve.

Group size
Groups of five.

What you need
Writing materials, photocopiable page 175 if required.

What to do
Explain to the class that they are to write a new television series set in a school. Since most writers base their stories on fact, the series they write will be based on their own school, class or group, but will also introduce some totally new characters. Each person in the group will be responsible for inventing one of the following characters:
- the new teacher;
- the class bully;
- the teacher's pet;
- the brainiest kid in the class
- the naughtiest kid in the class.

Tell the children to use pictures from clothing catalogues or magazines to find a person who fits their idea of the character they are going to create. They must write a detailed description of their character so that the casting director can find the right person for the part. The description should indicate the character's looks and personality. Explain that it is the 'quirks' of personality that often make people interesting and different. Discuss stereotypes and warn against making characters appear two-dimensional; even the worst person has some good in them!

Once finished, the writing should be read and discussed with the group.

Further activity
The children could write about what happens when the different characters meet. (See Chapter 4, Activity 15 for ideas on how this might be done.)

They could make a time-line of each character's day, detailing what they do hour by hour on both a school day and a non-school day.

2. First impressions

Age range
Nine to twelve.

Group size
Groups of five.

What you need
Writing materials.

What to do
Discuss the idea that we all interpret situations differently, depending on our previous

experience and personality. Ask the children to think of examples of this, and provide some yourself. This diversity of opinion makes life rich and interesting, but it also causes wars! Writers must know how their characters relate to each other and how they are likely to interpret and respond to various new situations.

After the first day at school, each character writes in her diary how she feels about the day and about each of the main characters she has met. It may help to provide a starter sentence ('Teacher: Started at my new school today. I must say that my new class are....' or 'Child: Back to school today. I'm in a new class and the new teacher seems to be...').

Once they have finished the first drafts, the group should read and discuss the responses one at a time, checking that they are broadly in character, and noting the aims and aspirations each character has for the new term. When the group are satisfied, the children should copy out their final drafts and display them.

3. Dealing with the bully

Age range
Nine to twelve.

Group size
Groups of five.

What you need
Writing material.

What to do
Bullying is, unhappily, something with which many children are familiar, and imaginative writing can provide an excellent way of

working through problems of this sort which occur in real life.

Explain to the class that authors often base their writing on experiences they have had, but change some details and exaggerate others until the end result is unrecognisable. Before writing an episode for television about bullying, the children must first explore their own attitudes and feelings about the subject.

Each child should first write about one occasion when he was bullied, or can remember someone else being bullied. He should include:
• how the incident started;
• what happened;
• how he felt;
• what happened to the bully and the victim.

The children should discuss their writing, and each child should write two reasons why he thinks bullies behave in this way. As a group, the children should share their reasons and list the five most important factors.

Once they have done this, the group should decide on a story outline for their television episode on bullying. It may be based on a real-life incident, an imaginary incident or a combination of the two. Once the outline has been decided by the group, however, each individual must write up his own version of the episode.

Further activity
Each group should discuss how they think bullies should be dealt with. The groups can then bring two of the best suggestions to a class discussion, which could formulate a class policy on bullying.

4. Behaving out of character

Age range
Nine to twelve.

Group size
Groups of five.

What you need
Writing materials.

What to do
The children will readily recognise that people's character traits mean that they generally behave in a fairly predictable fashion. They will probably be able to cite examples of this from situations that have arisen at home and school.

Discuss why this should be so, and ask if the children can think of any examples where people have behaved 'out of character' and done something which, for them, is totally surprising. Explore the reasons why people are sometimes impelled to act uncharacteristically.

All five children in the group should take their original television character and describe an imaginary incident in school where this character behaves in an uncharacteristic fashion. They should indicate why this happens, how the other characters react and whether the character involved is aware of the reaction to his or her surprising behaviour. The children should be encouraged to plan an outline of the story before they start writing.

The group's finished work can be combined so that each episode occurs on a different day, to provide a week in the life of the school.

Further activity
The stories can be read and discussed by different groups. Perhaps the children could write a short critique in the style of a television critic, commenting on what they like about another group's series so far.

5. Who dropped the stink-bomb?

Age range
Nine to twelve.

Group size
Groups of five.

What you need
Writing materials.

What to do
Explain that an inspector has come to see the school. Unfortunately, as she visits this class, the teacher gets notice of an urgent phone message. The inspector insists that the teacher should go to the phone and that she will look after the class in the meantime. On returning to the classroom, the teacher can smell an awful smell and the inspector is shouting at the class at the top of her voice; someone has let off a stink-bomb. The telephone message was about a sick relative and the teacher has had permission from the headteacher to leave immediately. She promises to sort the incident out by letter, and to find out who was responsible for dropping the stink-bomb. One thing is certain; it *wasn't* the naughtiest child, who is away with a bad cold.

One child in the group should take responsibility for writing about what exactly

happened after the teacher left the room.

The others should take the part of the teacher and each write a letter from the teacher to a different character asking what happened and explaining why the teacher is particularly disappointed in that person for not naming the culprit(s) immediately, as well as saying why he or she should now tell the whole truth.

The letters and the description of the incident should be displayed and read to the group. Each member of the group could choose a different letter and write the character's response.

6. The old house

Age range
Nine to twelve.

Group size
Groups of five.

What you need
Writing materials.

What to do
Explain that the teacher decides to take the class on a weekend break. The hotel turns out to be an old house set in its own grounds. The group must write a description of the old house for the scene builder and sound effects department. Each child will be responsible for describing one area:
• the banqueting hall;
• the old staircase;
• the bedrooms;
• the outside of the house;
• the reception area.

The children must list the furnishings in each area, with an emphasis on how they help to create an atmosphere. They should also consider how the lighting can contribute to the overall effect. Each child should then write one paragraph describing how the room or area looks and feels.

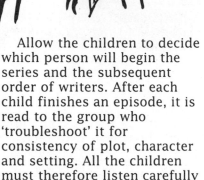

7. The holiday

Age range
Nine to twelve.

Group size
Groups of five.

What you need
Writing materials.

What to do
Explain that the class discovers that long ago, a horrible event occurred in the old house, and it is said to be haunted.

The groups are going to write five episodes about the adventures which their characters have at the old house. They should be linked together and must therefore be written in serial form.

The writing rules which must be established at the beginning of the writing process are:
• each episode must finish at a cliff-hanging point;
• each new episode begins with the last two sentences of the previous one;
• each writer should include the area he or she described in the last activity.

Allow the children to decide which person will begin the series and the subsequent order of writers. After each child finishes an episode, it is read to the group who 'troubleshoot' it for consistency of plot, character and setting. All the children must therefore listen carefully to each episode. Remind them how to make positive criticism.

8. The final day

Age range
Nine to twelve.

Group size
Groups of five.

What you need
Writing and drawing materials, card, adhesive, collage materials.

What to do
Explain that the last episode requires one member of each group to produce a piece of writing on which the final episode will be based. Choose a volunteer from each group and allow them some class-time in which to do the work before the whole-class session.

Explain to the volunteers that what they are about to be told is *top secret* and should not be revealed to anyone. Tell them that the teacher is leaving the school. They alone must decide:
• why the teacher is going;
• how the teacher feels about going;
• what the teacher will miss most about the class and why.

They are responsible for writing the teacher's leaving speech to the class. (Ways of teaching the children to do this can be found in Chapter 9, Activity 17.)

When the speeches have been written, they should be copied out, ready to be read to the rest of the group.

The class session should begin with each group member selecting a pupil character to represent. The volunteer should then read his or her speech to the group. Each character should jot down words to describe how they feel upon receiving the news. These reactions should be shared and discussed with the rest of the group.

Then each character must design and make a leaving card for the teacher. The cards are to remind the teacher about the individuals in the class and should reflect the personality of each character. Inside, the children should write a personal note to the teacher from their character, describing how that character felt on hearing the news.

Further activities
• The children could do some research to discover the evening and time when it would be most suitable to screen the series.
• Advertisements, trailers and covers for television magazines can be designed.

CHAPTER 6

Personal writing

Any writing in which children record their experiences, express their opinions or attitudes, describe their feelings or emotions or attempt to persuade others can be described as personal writing.

In a classroom in which children's development is encouraged, a high priority is always given to reflection upon personal experience. Teachers who value children's opinions, ideas and thoughts demand a personal response in much of the work carried out in the classroom.

Such teachers recognise that people only understand themselves and the world through sharing, reflecting upon, analysing and exploring their experiences. It is important to allow children the time, space and opportunity to do this. It is also important to encourage them to empathise with the contributions of others.

Personal writing presents many challenges. Children have to be encouraged to consider their own experiences, reactions and thoughts. They must be able to impose a sense of order and structure upon their experience and organise their writing accordingly.

In teaching personal writing there are three main difficulties to overcome.
• A stimulus must be chosen which will encourage the children to react, to reflect more deeply on new experiences, or to look upon old ones with new eyes.

• The lesson must be structured to encourage a diversity of responses or thought. All too often children respond in the way that they think the teacher wants them to respond, rather than honestly writing their own opinions and reflections.
• A clear framework must be provided which helps the children to organise their thoughts and write them down, encouraging them to craft a piece of writing that is their own and could never have been written by anyone else.

ACTIVITIES

1. First day at school

Age range
Five to seven.

Group size
Individuals and pairs.

What you need
Writing and drawing materials, paper divided into quarters.

What to do
Ask the children to think carefully about their first day at school, and the preparations for that day. Can they remember when they first tried on their new school clothes? When and how they got their school shoes? Who took them to school for the first time? How they got there? Ask them if they can recall all the new and different things they did at school that day, what they liked best and what they liked least.

Ask each child to draw the two most important things that happened on that day. When they have done this, tell the children to show and explain their drawings to their neighbour. Allow four or five minutes for this, telling the children to swap half-way through this time. Tell them that they must listen very carefully to their partner because they may be asked to talk about his or her drawing to the rest of the class. At the end of this session, invite pairs of children to the front of the class and ask them to explain their partners' drawings. Invite the 'artist' to contribute any additional details that may have been omitted by their partner and encourage the rest of the class to ask questions too.

You may like to quickly write key statements about each picture as they arise during this session. These could be read to the class and displayed on the wall beside the pictures to which they refer.

2. Feeling ill

Age range
Five to seven.

Group size
Individuals.

What you need
Writing material, paper for zigzag books.

What to do
Begin this activity by telling the class about the last time that you felt ill. Tell the story in definite stages:
• realising that you were not well – what you were doing at the time, which parts of your body ached or hurt, and what happened when you told someone else about how you felt;
• being ill – how you felt and what you did;

• recovering from the illness and feeling a little better again.

As you tell the story, illustrate it with three drawings to make a zigzag book. Comment on the detail you are putting into each drawing, for example, the expression on your face, your body posture, background details, such as your bedroom wallpaper and pictures, and so on. Use as wide a vocabulary as possible to describe how you felt.

Ask the children to think about a recent time when they felt unwell. Again, concentrate on the three stages of being unwell. Ask all the children to tell a partner about what happened when they were ill and choose some individuals to share their experience with the whole class.

Give the children folded paper and pencils and explain how to write the zigzag books. While the children do this, circulate, asking individuals to tell you their story from the pictures they have drawn, and encouraging detailed drawings which attempt to indicate the different emotions and situations. Children who have difficulty with this should be encouraged to experiment with different expressions in front of a mirror. At the bottom of

each drawing write, or help the children to write, about what happened.

Once the zigzag books have been completed, the children should be given an opportunity to read their books to the others in the class.

3. Playgroup

Age range
Five to seven.

Group size
The whole class and individuals.

What you need
Writing and drawing materials, three small pieces and one large piece of paper per child, adhesive.

What to do
Talk to the class about the playgroup, nursery or childminder they went to

before they came to school. Ask them to tell you about the things they used to do that are different from the things they do now. Tell them to draw three things they used to like doing at their playgroup, one on each of the small pieces of paper. When they have done this, help them to stick their three drawings on to the larger piece of paper in the order, with the activity they liked best at the top. Label the activities 1, 2 and 3 and write a short sentence about each one, getting the child to copy-write it underneath.

Once finished, the work should be discussed in groups and displayed in the classroom.

4. Dreams and nightmares

Age range
Five to seven.

Group size
Individuals.

What you need
Writing and drawing materials, *Where the Wild Things Are* by Maurice Sendak (Bodley Head/ Puffin) or a similar book.

In my dream I could hear my BMX bike saying I want some Coacola and chips and burgurs as well because O'h and sorry I   a yogurt because I Want to be a tough bike and drive fast and eu'ven even do stunts

What to do
This activity can be introduced by reading the children a book such as *Where the Wild Things Are* by Maurice Sendak.

Children should be encouraged to talk and write about dreams and nightmares that they can remember, and also about what happened when they woke up. The idea of daydreams can also be introduced and their differences and similarities to night-time dreams discussed.

5. Tastes we like

Age range
Five to seven.

Group size
Groups of six to eight.

What you need
Photocopiable page 179, samples of the foods listed on it, writing materials.

What to do
Introduce the activity to the whole class by discussing what foods the children like and dislike eating. This should be used as an opportunity to introduce the many words used to describe the taste and texture of food. The children should be given plenty of opportunity to use and discuss these. There will probably be confusion about some vocabulary, for example, bitter and sour, crunchy and chewy, crisp and crunchy. Give the children samples of different types of food to look at and ask them to try to describe and identify them. Send most of the class off to draw a picture of their favourite meal, keeping back a small group to carry out a 'taste test'.

Explain to the group the idea of a 'taste test', whereby a child closes her eyes and is fed a small sample of food which she must try to describe and identify, saying what is pleasant or nasty about each one. Show the group how to use photocopiable page 179 to record the responses. Divide the group into pairs, with one child giving the other the samples and recording their verdict on the chart. Once one child in the pair has tasted all the food listed, plus one other chosen by the tester, they should change roles.

When the first group in a class has done this activity, it is useful for them to explain what they did to the rest of the class. This serves to introduce to subsequent groups both the new vocabulary and the idea of recording information in chart form, as well as being a good oral language activity for the original group.

Further activity
This activity can be followed with a visit from the school nurse or dentist to talk to the children about how to look after their teeth.

Should you want to explore the senses in greater depth, this activity can be adapted for the sense of touch using 'feely bags'.

6. Good smells, bad smells

Age range
Five to seven.

Group size
Groups of six to eight.

What you need
Display-sized writing materials, six to eight felt-tipped pens (different colours), one black pen for yourself, small containers with lids.

What to do
Ask each child in the group to tell you his favourite smell, and why he likes it. Write this information on to a large piece of display paper. Then do the same for the smells the children dislike.

Ask the children to brainstorm all the different smells they can think of, and write these on to a second sheet. Give each child a coloured pen and, together, make a key on the large piece of paper to show which child has which colour pen. Then ask the children to use their pens to place a tick or a cross beside each smell on the large sheet according to whether they like or dislike it. If a child really likes or violently dislikes anything, they could indicate this with a double tick or cross.

Further activity
Show the children how to make 'smell potions'. Explain that everything has a smell, but that some things only smell particularly strong when they have been ground up.

Demonstrate this with a piece of grass. Take the group outside, and ask each child to find a leaf or flower with a particularly nice smell. Once found, these should be ground up and placed in labelled containers and displayed for others to sniff.

7. Girls' toys, boys' toys

Age range
Five to seven.

Group size
Groups of six or eight (equal number of girls and boys in each group).

What you need
Catalogues with pictures of children's toys, scissors, six or eight sorting rings, paper (blank and headed – see below), writing materials, adhesive.

What to do
Give the children the catalogues of children's toys and allow them time to look at the pictures. Tell each child to choose nine different toys that he or she likes and to cut them out. (Nine is, of course, an arbitrary number and you could use this activity to reinforce any suitable number you wish).

Once each picture has been cut out, it should be stored in the child's sorting ring so that it doesn't get lost or muddled up with another's work. When the children have collected their nine pictures ask them to choose the best three, placing the rest into a group pile. These three pictures should then be stuck on to a piece of paper in order of preference. Each child should write '1' beside her favourite, '2' beside her second choice, and '3' beside her third choice.

Age range
Five to seven.

Group size
Individuals or pairs.

What you need
Writing materials, A4 paper and larger paper.

What to do
Ask the children to show you how they look when they laugh. Point out what happens to their mouth, eyebrows, cheeks and eyes. Ask them to pretend to cry and let them comment on what happens to their faces. Put the children into pairs and ask them to draw their partner either laughing or crying. Emphasise that they will have to look very carefully at their partner's face and draw exactly what they see. The drawings should be as detailed as possible. Once finished, they should be cut out and given to the subject, so that each child has a drawing of him or herself which has been done by another child.

Children should look at the drawing and try to remember the last time they laughed or cried. Where was it, and who was present? On the larger sheet of paper, they should draw the whole scene and write about it. The children's work should then be mounted and either displayed on the wall or made into a class book, with the portrait of each child next to the scene which prompted the laughter or tears.

Then each child must show her choice to the rest of the group and explain why she likes these toys.

Discuss the diversity, asking the children to explain why they didn't pick particular toys. It is very likely that they will explain that some toys are for girls and others are for boys. This notion should be discussed and explored further; can all toys be classified in this way, or are some seen as acceptable for both girls and boys? What do they think makes a toy suitable for girls or for boys? How do they recognise such a toy? Has anyone ever played with a toy that they think was really *meant* for the opposite sex? Did they enjoy it?

Give each child a piece of paper divided into three sections headed 'Girls' toys', 'Boys' toys' and 'Toys for everyone'. Ask the children to look at the discarded pictures in the middle and to try to find two toys which they think are good examples to stick into each section. Discuss the examples that the children choose, trying to ask questions that will encourage them to think beyond the stereotypes and to recognise the complex realities.

After this session, give the children time to explore toys which were classified as being for the opposite sex only. Allow a 'familiarisation period' and give plenty of encouragement and time to this part of the activity. Ask if they can find two good things about the toy. Afterwards, discuss what the children did and whether their views of the toy have changed. If so, these changes could be represented on the written work with arrows to indicate the new section into which the toy should be placed.

I like to hug my Mum. I hugged my Mum this morning.

9. Hugging makes us feel better

Age range
Five to seven.

Group size
Individuals.

What you need
Writing materials.

What to do
Ask the children to draw a picture of two people or objects they like to hug. These might be parents, grandparents, friends, siblings, toys, pets, special blankets, pillows, and so on. Ask them to show their pictures to the rest of the class and discuss how it feels to hug and to be hugged, and also when they most feel the need for a hug.

Ask the children to write about the last time they hugged the two things they have drawn.

10. First impressions

Age range
Seven to nine.

Group size
Individuals.

What you need
Writing materials.

What to do
Tell the children to choose one of their friends to think about. Ask the class to remember the first time they met their friend; where they were, what the weather was like, what they were each wearing, what they were doing, what their friend was doing, how they first noticed their friend, how they got talking to each other, the first thing they said, the first thing their friend said, and so on.

Encourage the children to be as specific as possible. Children will generally have very clear memories of this and will be keen to describe them, often reminding each other of details long since forgotten. If anyone can't remember, or hasn't got a best friend, encourage them to choose someone in the class that they can remember meeting for the first time, even if they are not particular friends.

Once the scene has been firmly remembered, ask the children what they first thought about their friend. Did they know from the start that they would get on, or were they wary of each other? Why did they start talking or playing together?

Ask the children to write all these things down, emphasising the importance of the details and encouraging them not to worry too much about spelling or neatness at this stage. You may choose to put key 'reminder' questions on the board, or simply trust each child to write the most vivid memories and impressions first.

Once finished, the writing can be copied out, and perhaps a photograph or drawing added.

We have always found that if this work is made into a book and displayed in the classroom, it is repeatedly read by the children and greeted with enthusiasm and interest by their parents.

11. New starts, secret promises

Age range
Seven to eleven.

Group size
Individuals.

What you need
One small, empty matchbox per child, sticky tape, writing materials.

What to do
This is a particularly good activity to do when the class has been together for about a term and the children know each other reasonably well.

After a short holiday, or at particular points in the year, it is useful to take stock and resolve to make a new start in various areas of our lives; adults often go on diets or resolve to keep cupboards tidy, for example. Explain this to the children and ask them to look within themselves and to think of an area of their character that they would like to improve. Perhaps they don't like sharing sweets, or are mean to a classmate.

Give the children several examples of promises that might be made for the months ahead. This must be done in a very serious way. Stress that the promise should be specific to one area, so that it can be concentrated upon. Ask each child to write or draw his promise on to a single sheet of paper that is immediately folded and placed inside his own matchbox. No one except the child will read the promise, or know what it is about.

The matchboxes should now be covered, sealed and beautifully decorated. They will never be opened and their contents will always remain a secret. Once finished, stick the boxes around the entrance to the classroom with double-sided sticky tape. As children walk in or out of the classroom each day, they must look at their own box and remember their promise.

12. My first stories

Age range
Seven to eleven.

Group size
Individuals.

What you need
Story books for a much younger age range, writing materials.

What to do
This activity will require two sessions.

First session
Spread the books out on the floor or table and give the class an opportunity to look at the front covers, but do not let them open the books at this stage. Ask if anyone recognises any particular book or story, following this up with questions about when they first saw it, whether they read it themselves or had it read to them (if so, by whom, when and where), and so on. If they do not recognise *any* of the books or stories, they should think about one which they do remember.

Allow the children some time just to read the books (this may take *quite* some time!). Collect the books together again and give the children ten minutes to reminisce in pairs about the first books they had, or stories they can remember. Stress that the small details and memories are important and that they should try to be honest about what they thought at the time. Then, give the children a limited time to write everything down as quickly as possible. This should be done with the whole class working individually and in silence.

At the end of this session, ask the children to hand their work in, but stress that this is only so that you can help with spellings; you will not be marking it as a 'finished product'. Accordingly, correct the spellings but do not worry about the grammar, handwriting, punctuation or order.

Second session
The second session should take place within a couple of days of the first. At the start, explain to the class that you have corrected all the spellings in their written work, but little else since this is a first draft. Return the work and begin the lesson with three or four minutes silence while they read it.

Explain that you want them to use their first draft as the basis for a piece of personal writing entitled 'My first stories'. They should use the memories they have written down, but they can elaborate on some of them or change the wording or order if they wish. Ask the children to pay particular attention to their opening sentence and ban the use of 'My first stories were...' as an opening. You could suggest that the children write three different beginnings and then choose the best.

13. Heroes and heroines

Age range
Eight to twelve.

Group size
Individuals.

What you need
Writing and drawing materials.

What to do
Ask the children to individually list all the people they consider to be a true hero or heroine. Beside each name, ask them to write the important characteristics which, in their eyes, qualify each choice. They should also say whether each characteristic is essential, very important or quite important and why. These choices should be shared, either in pairs or with the rest of the class. The children must be made to justify their opinions.

After the discussion, the lists should be used as the basis for a piece of writing with the working title of 'My heroes and heroines'. Children should choose whether to focus on the personalities they

have identified, using their lists of qualities to write about why these people are true heroes or heroines, or to focus on the characteristics which they think are important and write about what their ideal hero or heroine would be like. In their writing, they should justify their opinions. Tell the class that although the working title can be 'Heroes and heroines', they should decide on another title for their own work once they have finished it.

Further activity
Discuss the traditional tales in which the true 'goody' is not recognised as such until the very end. Ask the children in pairs to list the important attributes of such a person, and to find *one* child in the class who has each attribute. Although some children will undoubtedly have more than one attribute, they should be cited only once.

14. Christkindl

Age range
Eight to twelve.

Group size
Individuals.

What you need
Writing materials, box or hat.

What to do
Christkindl is a German Christmas custom which can be introduced into the class. Every child should place his or her name into a hat. In enormous secrecy, each child draws out a name, until each child has the name of a classmate. This is his or her 'Christ-child', or Christkindl.

For the weeks of advent leading up to the Christmas holiday, each child must do a good turn each day for their Christkindl. The activity works best if secrecy is maintained throughout so that no one knows who is bound to do them good deeds, which might range from small gifts, such as a biscuit left secretly in a desk, to a bit of help with work or some other small kindness. Each good deed should be written every day on a special list that is kept, decorated and eventually presented to the child as a Christmas present on the last day of term.

15. Choosing illustrations

Age range
Eight to twelve.

Group size
Pairs.

What you need
Illustrated books of traditional tales (as many different styles as possible), writing materials.

What to do
Select a couple of books, preferably about the same tale, but with radically different styles of illustration. Show them to the children and ask for their reactions and opinions. The children should be asked to comment on what is good about each style. Encourage them to think about what each illustration adds to the story. Does it help the reader to select the book, shape her imagination, or add details which are not described in the print?

Tell the children about the job of an illustrator and how

he or she must choose which parts of the story to illustrate, the detail to include and the style and size of the pictures. Show them where to find the name of the illustrator on the front cover and title page. Then give the class ten minutes to examine the illustrations in some of the other books you have selected.

Put the class into working pairs and ask them to select one book which they feel has been well illustrated. Children should be encouraged to justify their own opinions and to argue their case. Tell the children to find the name of the illustrator and to write a letter to him or her saying why they personally like the drawings so much.

Further activity
By now the class should appreciate how difficult it is to be an illustrator. Read the class

a story, preferably one which they will not have heard before. Either select one part for each child to illustrate, or ask them each to select a part. Then produce a class version of the story, complete with illustrations, title page and front and back cover design.

16. Personal reactions

Age range
Seven to nine.

Group size
Individuals.

What you need
Photographs cut from magazines (enough for one between two), 'prompt' questions on the board (covered up initially).

What to do
Give each pair of children one picture to share. They are not to discuss it, but should spend two minutes in total silence studying it. Then ask the children to put the picture face

down on the desk and turn to face someone who is sitting near them, but who has not seen their picture. Each child should be given five minutes to describe the picture and how it made him feel. They should focus on the following questions, which should be already written out on the board and can now be uncovered:
• What did you notice first?
• What did you first think about the picture and why?
• What thoughts did you have while examining the details?
• Why do you think the photograph was taken?

Tell the children that these are 'prompt' questions; they don't have to stick to them exclusively. Their partner can ask questions about their photograph or their reaction. (You may need to discuss what sorts of questions would be most helpful.)

The class should then write about the photographs and their reactions to them. You should point out the different ways in which their writing could begin:
• with a straight description of the photograph, leading into their reaction;
• with their reaction, leading back to the photograph;
• with their perception of the photographer and the motivation behind the photograph.

Emphasise that it is up to the writer how the writing should start. Allow the class time to write individual pieces of work. Only when it is

finished should the children share their work with the child who is writing about the same photograph.

Once they have finished, each pair of children should mount and display their pieces of work beside the photograph to which they refer.

17. Dreams of glory

Age range
Eight to twelve.

Group size
Individuals.

What you need
Writing materials, introductory reading (not essential).

What to do
A short passage from *Billy Liar* by Keith Waterhouse may serve as a good introduction to the idea that we all secretly dream of suddenly stepping into the limelight and triumphing in some way; perhaps winning an Olympic gold medal, or replacing the lead singer of a pop group. All dreams are different. A few may be attainable, but most are not. It is important to explore this idea orally and to encourage the feeling that dreams are precious and must be respected.

Do not expect children to tell others about current dreams, but most won't mind sharing a dream that they used to have. Perhaps you could tell the class about your secret dreams of glory too!

Ask the children to think of a dream of personal triumph that they are prepared to share with the class and to write a short paragraph to describe the moment of glory for which they long, and the events leading up to it.

This writing should be discussed with one other person, who should ask questions about the situation described. After redrafting, the work should be copied on to a piece of cloud-shaped paper, to make an attractive display on the wall. Children should be allowed to choose whether or not to put their name on this piece of work.

18. A personal triumph

Age range
Eight to twelve.

Group size
Groups of five to six.

What you need
Writing materials.

What to do
Introduce the lesson by saying that some dreams can never be realised. However, we all experience smaller triumphs in our lives. These are often very personal and even though the achievement may seem tiny to others, it is how it feels to the individual that is important. You could illustrate this point with a story about yourself or with an extract from a suitable novel.

Ask the children to think of a small triumph of their own. Give them a few minutes to think, and then ask them to write rough notes about the triumph itself at the bottom of a sheet of paper. Each child should then share this with the group, who can ask questions in order to clarify the story.

Working from the top of the paper, ask the children to note in rough the sequence of events leading up to the triumph. At each stage, the children should consider the following points:
• where they were;
• which other people were involved;
• how they felt;
• what happened.

My triumpho by Laura Smith Age 9.

I think most of my triumphs were achieved in swimming. They include my first jump off a high board in the swimming-baths, managing to swim front-crawl, and getting into the relay in our school gala.

My biggest triumph was when I learnt to ride my bike without stabilisers. I must of been about four or five years old when it happened. I remember being outside in the big square near our house, I was riding round in circles when I saw some boys showing off because they didn't use stabilisers, so I got off my bike, bent down and started pulling at my stabilisers, I think that I soon realised that I would have to unscrew them. My big brother Cameron helped me and soon I was riding up and down the square, I fell off at first but soon I got the hang of it. I went home and shouted for mum.

I was still a bit wobbly the next day but I felt great, the boys I had seen stopped showing off and went away. Inside me I thanked them because they had been the cause of it all.

Using this as a rough draft, the children should then write a short piece describing the moment of triumph. Finally, the writing can be displayed on star-shaped pieces of paper.

It is very important to remember that children will only be prepared to read their writing to the class if the atmosphere is supportive. The children's privacy must be respected if they prefer not to have these rather private thoughts and ideas displayed for all to read.

19. Personal descriptions

Age range
Nine to twelve.

Group size
Individuals.

What you need
Drawing materials (not essential), writing materials.

What to do
The writing session should be preceded with a close-observation drawing lesson. Sit each child opposite a friend or partner and give them two minutes in silence to look carefully at each other. Tell them to look at the shape of the face, the way the hair falls, the distinguishing features, the type of nose and so on. Then give one child in each pair 15 minutes to draw his partner, putting in as much detail as possible. After 15 minutes, tell them to swap roles. (If they haven't finished tell them not to worry; the drawings can be perfected at a later stage.)

Ask them to think about how their partner looks when he or she is in the playground. How does the hair, expression, facial lines, slope of the shoulders differ?

Explain that you are going to describe someone in the class. The children must listen without saying anything until the end of your description, when they will be asked who you were talking about. Make sure that you describe how physical aspects change, for example, 'Her fringe is quite long and straight, so it often falls in front of her eyes. She has a habit of flicking it back by tossing her head...' or 'His hair is short and black. When he has been running and is hot and sweaty, he wipes his forehead and his fringe sticks straight up in the air...'.

Encourage the children to take turns describing their partners, emphasising that they must describe habitual actions as well as physical appearances and how these alter in different environments. When they understand what sort of detail you want, tell them to write descriptions of their partners.

20. Favourite tales

Age range
Nine to twelve.

Group size
Individuals or pairs.

What you need
Writing materials.

What to do
Explain to the class that a particular publisher needs to find out what sort of stories children like, to help with the planning of a compilation book. The children can help with this valuable piece of

research. Explain that the class will be divided in half, and each half will provide very different (but equally important) kinds of evidence for the 'editor-in-chief'.

Ask the whole class to brainstorm all the traditional tales they can think of. Then divide the class in half and send one half away so that each child can choose his or her four favourite tales and list them in order of preference. They must do this without consultation, but warn them that they should be prepared to justify both their chosen tales and their order of preference.

Gather the other half of the class closely around you, so that the writers are not distracted. Explain that they are to act as investigators, questioning the writers about their lists to find out why they chose each tale and why they placed them in this particular order.

This group should ask as wide a variety of questions as possible, trying all the time to work out a 'personal profile' for their partner. They should probe to find out which decisions were easy and which

were harder to make, what makes a particular child like a story and what bores him, what he considers the most important aspects of a good tale, and so on. Emphasise that this is a skilled and difficult task because the investigator will have to suspend her own judgements and preferences in order to understand those of the list writer.

Ask each child in the 'investigator' group to pair with a list writer. Allow 15 minutes for the investigation to take place (remembering to warn the children half way through and a few minutes before the end). Then separate the pairs and ask the list writers to write about why they chose the stories they did and why they put them in that order.

The investigators should be asked to write a more general piece about what makes a good story, using evidence gained from the interview and from

their own opinions. This is quite a difficult piece of writing and the investigators may need some help to decide how to structure their work. Depending on your teaching style, you may choose to:
• involve all the investigators in a discussion (listing salient points on the chalkboard);
• help the investigators either individually or in groups by discussing possible starting points and how these could be followed through.

Further activity
This work should definitely be read to the rest of the class and discussed. The children could send copies of their work to a publisher, along with an explanatory letter (see Chapter 2 on functional writing for ideas about how to teach this). The originals would make an eye-catching display.

21. A work journal

Age range
Nine to twelve.

Group size
Individuals.

What you need
Writing materials.

What to do
The children who are most successful socially and academically in school are those who can monitor and take responsibility for their own education in partnership with parents and teachers. It is important, therefore, that we evolve teaching strategies which foster a sense of academic progress and encourage children to become independent learners.

Explain to the class that a work journal is a personal notebook in which pupils evaluate their own performance at school socially and academically. When introducing the idea to the children, it may be helpful to give them the following headings for the front of their journal in order to help them structure their thinking and writing.

This week
• Which two pieces of work do you think you did best this week?
• Why were these pieces so successful?
• Which pieces of work did you enjoy doing most, and why?
• Was there any work you didn't understand this week? (What did you do about this? Where did you go for help? Did you understand it eventually?)

This Week

The piece of work I think I did best this week was in art. We were printing our faces onto a t-shirt. The piece of work was successful because I am quite good at art and it was quite easy. The pieces of work I enjoyed doing most was in English when I had make a poem about an imaginary creature. I enjoyed working in a group and making an advert and the teacher videoed our adverts. I enjoyed doing this because it was fun but it made us realise how long an advert on tv takes to make everything perfect. In maths I didn't understand a sum so I asked the teacher and she explained it to me and I eventually understood it. I helped someone in p.e. this week to do a handstand. My help was success____ she ca___ do a

• Did you help anyone this week? (Was your help successful?)
• Did you cause or take part in any arguments?
• Write three things you learned in school this week.
• What was the highlight of the week for you in school? (Why?)

The plan for next week
• What things should you attend to next week in order to improve?
• Name one particular subject to concentrate on next week.
• Choose one person to whom you will be kinder.
• If there is something that you need to tell the teacher in order to be happier or get on better with your work, leave a note on his desk before leaving school today.

This activity, carried out regularly, gives pupils a focus for evaluating their performance in school and provides a forum for child and teacher to share in future planning. A direct yet informal line of communication is opened up by the final activity on the sheet, which may be invaluable.

It is not advisable for the structure provided above to be followed for more than a few weeks, or what should be a thoughtful, personal response could very easily become just another exercise answered mechanically without any real consideration or care. This will not happen, however, if both the teacher and the child take the consultation process seriously.

On a Monday, children should look at their journals at the start of the day, checking their resolves and plans for the week ahead.

Each week, appointments must be made to meet several children when journals will be read and academic and social progress discussed. This is the teacher's opportunity to share the planning process with the child, to reinforce success and introduce strategies to overcome difficulties.

CHAPTER 7

Personal writing in a context

This chapter provides various contexts through which the children can be encouraged to express their opinions and emotions. The contexts provided are divided into sections for the age ranges five to seven, seven to nine and nine to twelve.

Through topic work on 'Ourselves', the children can be encouraged to reflect on their relationships with others and to become aware of lifestyles that are different from their own.

The topic for seven- to nine-year-olds provides an opportunity to think about holidays, leading to the wider theme of defining work and leisure.

Finally, the theme of 'School' should provide older children with a chance to consider their whole attitude to school, concentrating both on how their feelings have changed since they started school and on issues that may be more current. The topic will also encourage them to analyse their reactions and opinions.

Personal writing in a context   93

ACTIVITIES

Ourselves

These activities for five-to seven-year-olds focus on the children's home life, family and friends.

1. How we spend the day

Age range
Five to seven.

Group size
Six to eight.

What you need
Writing materials, paper for zigzag books.

What to do
Many children can become quite worried about how their parents spend the day while they are at school. Sometimes it helps to discuss this in an open and reassuring situation, making it clear that during school hours their parents, while not being lonely, think of them often. It is also important for children of this age to discuss the different ways in which people they know spend their time.

Begin by discussing how the children spend the day. If you were to walk into their homes before school, what would they be doing? What do they do when they are at school? What about after school?

Do the children's older or younger siblings spend their day in the same way? What about their grandparents, and the other adults they know? (Children often have very interesting ideas about what teachers and headteachers do when they are not at school!)

Tell the children that they are going to make a three-page zigzag book about their own day, and show them how to do this. Suggest that it would be interesting to find out about what their parents do during the day, and that maybe they could ask their mum or dad (or any other adult of their choosing) to make a similar zigzag book to show this. They could then bring this book in to school and share it with the rest of the class.

At home-time, give the children some blank paper for making the zigzag book and remind them that they will have to explain to their parents what they need to do. (You may decide also to send a covering letter.) Suggest that maybe the children could show their own book to their parents as an example of what is required.

When the books are brought in to school from home they should all be displayed and, over a period of time, each child should be encouraged to read both her own and her parent's book to the other children in the class.

2. Special people

Age range
Five to seven.

Group size
Individuals.

What you need
Photographs of parents or carers, writing materials.

What to do
Either ask the children to bring in a photograph of their mum or dad or carer, or photograph some of them as they deliver or collect their children from school. Show the photographs to the class and ask each child to think of one special thing that makes their own mum or

dad or carer different from anyone else's. You could ask them what makes their parent or carer stand out from a crowd of other adults. Help them to write about the things that make their mum, dad or carer especially special.

When this is done, the work should be mounted alongside the photograph and made into a class book entitled 'Our special people'.

Further activity
If the parents or carers responded well to making zigzag books, ask them to contribute to a book about children in the class. Ask them each to write three short, simple sentences saying what is special about their child and to send this, along with a photograph of the child, to school. These can then be mounted and made into a class book entitled 'We are special'.

3. My bedroom

Age range
Five to seven.

Group size
Individuals or pairs.

What you need
Painting materials, writing materials.

What to do
Ask the children each to think about their bedroom at home. Split the children into pairs, and ask them to tell their partner all about their bedroom. They must be sure to include as much detail as possible.

Lucy

Lucy is very good at telling jokes and making us all laugh.
Lucy is very kind to her Gran
Lucy always eats her dinner.
from her Mum and Dad

• Do they share the room? If so, do they like sharing it, and how did they decide which bed to have?
• What toys do they always keep in their bedroom?
• Where are their things stored?
• What is their bed like?
• Do they have any special pictures?
• Are there rules about keeping the bedroom tidy?
Ask them if their bedroom has ever been changed or reorganised, and if so, why and how. Are there perhaps some things they would like to change about their room, and if so, what? Choose a few children to briefly tell the rest of the class about their bedroom.

Now ask the children to paint pictures of their bedrooms, trying to portray them exactly as they are. When this has been done, each child should write about his room.

Sometimes, when doing this activity, the children have more to say than they are able to put down on paper. Help them to write the most important things themselves and scribe, or ask another adult to scribe, the other details for them.

Each child should be asked to show his picture and talk about or read what he has have written to the class before it is displayed on the wall.

4. My whole family

Age range
Five to seven.

Group size
Individuals.

What you need
Writing and drawing materials, flashcards of family relationship words.

What to do
Young children often have quite complicated home situations and get confused about the notions of 'family' and 'household'. Grandparents, aunts and uncles, divorced or separated parents may all be family, although they often do not live in the same house as the child. Others, who might live in the same house, may

> my best friend is Eleanor because she has good games to play and we play comedy games and they are brilliant games and when I hurt myself and she helps me to write words and she comes round to my house and sometimes we both hurt ourselfs we laugh because we bump our heads together and it is funny and her favorite thing is writting.
>
> Lorna Smith

not be family, for example au pairs, lodgers and guests. Through discussion, the child can often come to understand the wider meaning of the term 'family' and begin to resolve any personal conflicts and misunderstandings.

Ask the children to draw a house-shaped box in the centre of their paper. Inside it they should draw all the people with whom they live. Beside each figure, help the children to write the name of each person and their relationship to them. Now ask them to think of other relations that do not live with them. Around the outside of the paper, get them to draw the set of people in each household, putting a house-shaped box around those who live together. The name of each person and their relationship to the child should be written beside each drawing.

The children can draw arrows from their house to those of their relatives, showing by what means they would travel were they to visit them.

The children should be given an opportunity to explain and discuss their drawings within a group. It is important that they realise that all families are different and that there is no universal 'family type'. They should be allowed to recognise, discuss and accept the similarities and differences that exist.

Further activity
The children can write about their memories of a special visit to see one set of relatives.

5. My special toy

Age range
Five to seven.

Group size
Individuals.

What you need
A toy, writing and drawing materials.

What to do
Ask the children to think of a special toy. Explain that this should not be their newest or latest toy, but one that they have had for some time and of which they are particularly fond. Arrange for a few children each day to bring their toy to school to show the class and tell them about why it is special. On the day that each child does this, teach them how to do a close-observation drawing of their toy, first looking at it very carefully and pointing out all the distinctive features which should then be represented in their drawing. Help the children to produce a short piece of writing which explains what is special about this toy and why they like it so much.

6. Friends, arguments and saying sorry

Age range
Five to seven.

Group size
Individuals.

What you need
Writing materials.

What to do
This activity requires two sessions.

First session
Ask the children each to talk about one friend, saying why they like him or her, what games they play together and so on. In the first session they should write about this person.

Second session
For the second session, ask the children to think of a time when they had an argument with this friend, or thought their friend behaved unkindly towards them. If they are able, ask them to write about how the argument or incident started and what happened. Ask them to read their work to the group and to talk about it. Why did they say and do the things that they did, and how did they really feel? Talk about what happened in the end and how the argument or disagreement was resolved.

Encourage the children to think of all the different ways of saying sorry to someone.

Children often have special playground rituals for this and they will also be able to draw on experience from home. (If it is appropriate, take the opportunity to point out that parents still love their children, even when they are cross with them!)

With the group, make a list about how they feel when they have argued with a friend and discuss why they feel like this. Finally, the children can be asked to finish their writing by saying how the argument was resolved and what they think of it now, when they remember it.

7. A special family day

Age range
Five to seven.

Group size
Individuals.

What you need
Photographs, writing materials.

What to do
Ask the children to try to bring in a photograph of a special day that they can remember having with their family. Ask them to talk, draw and write about the clothes they wore, where they went and why, how they felt about the outing, what they expected it to be like and what it was actually like. Display the written work in the classroom beside the photograph.

Holidays

These activities for seven- to nine-year-olds provide an opportunity for the children to reflect on their previous experience of successful and unsuccessful holidays and to think more deeply about the meaning of the word 'holiday'.

1. What is a holiday?

Age range
Seven to nine.

Group size
Individuals.

What you need
Writing materials, children's photographs.

What to do
Ask the children to tell you what the word 'holiday' means to them. They will have many different definitions and will be divided, for example, about how long a break has to be to become a holiday and whether it is possible to have a holiday at home, a holiday alone or a working holiday. Try to establish the broadest possible definition of a holiday. Ask them if it is possible not to enjoy a holiday, or does the experience then cease to be a holiday? Do they consider it possible for an animal to have a holiday and does this depend on the type of animal? (If a cat can have a holiday, could a mouse or a spider?)

Ask the class to brainstorm all the essential and non-essential features of a holiday and list them on the board. Individuals should then select and prioritise the most important ten features, finally comparing their list with a partner, noting similarities and differences.

Children should then be asked to write a very short piece entitled 'What is a holiday?' They should use the essential features they have identified and justify their decisions.

Once the writing has been finished, the children should choose how to mount and display their writing under a heading which indicates the many different occasions that can be defined as a holiday.

2. Mini-holidays

Age range
Seven to nine.

Group size
Individuals.

What you need
Writing materials.

What to do
This activity should be done over several days.

Before the children leave school one Friday, ask them to spend the weekend thinking about the shortest holiday they have ever enjoyed. Explain that this may be a day spent at home or an outing that only lasted a morning. They should come prepared to tell the class about it the following week. If they wish, they can bring in pictures, souvenirs or notes to help them.

The activity works best if the children are asked to sign up for 'appointment times', which are spread over the course of a week, when the children know they will be required to share their mini-holiday story with the rest of the class. During each talk, scribe the child's ideas in note form. When all the children have talked about their holidays, they will be able to use your notes as a 'first draft' for a piece of writing.

Once the children are ready to do the writing, give out all your scribed pieces of work. Explain that these are very rough, but the children should be able to use them as a starting point for their own piece of work.

The first thing they must do is read your notes and think again about their holiday. They should decide on a title for

their work and read through your notes again to decide how to begin. They should be encouraged to omit, alter or expand on any ideas they wish, and to mark their alterations on to your script. When they are happy with the writing, the work should be copied and compiled into a class book.

3. Holiday photographs

Age range
Seven to nine.

Group size
Individuals or pairs.

What you need
Writing materials, children's photographs, question cards.

What to do
Arrange for the children to bring a holiday photograph into school on a specific day.

The photograph should not just be a scenic view but must be of people that they know or remember.

Divide the class into working pairs, with one set of question-prompt cards between them. The cards should say things like:
• When and where was the photograph taken?
• Who are the people in the photograph?
• Who took the photograph and why?
• What were your thoughts and feelings towards the people in the picture?
• What happened before or after the photograph was taken?
• Why was the day special?
• How did it begin or end?

Emphasise that these are prompt questions and should not be slavishly adhered to by the questioner; they may be added to or omitted as circumstances dictate. Give each child 15 minutes to find

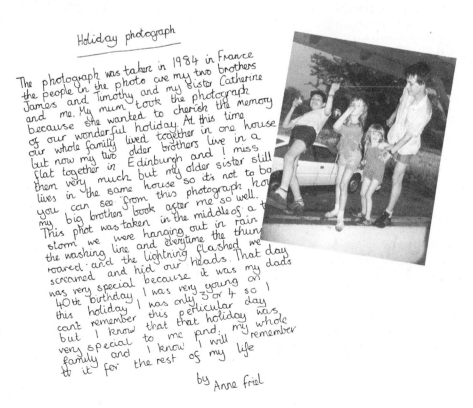

Holiday photograph

The photograph was taken in 1984 in France the people in the photo are my two brothers James and Timothy and my sister Catherine and me. My mum took the photograph because she wanted to cherish the memory of our wonderful holiday. At this time our whole family lived together in one house but now my two older brothers live in a flat together in Edinburgh and I miss them very much but my older sister still lives in the same house so it's not to bad you can see from this photograph how my big brothers book after me so well. This phot was taken in the middle of a t storm we were hanging out in rain the washing line and everytime the thun roared and the lightning flashed we screamed and hid our heads. That day was very special because it was my dads 40th birthday. I was very young on this holiday I was only 3 or 4 so I cant remember this perticular day but I know that that holiday was very special to me and: my whole family and I know I will remember th it for the rest of my life

by Anne Friel

out about her partner's photograph. At the end of the 15 minute period, the questioner must nominate the five questions which prompted the most interesting answers. These will then be used by the photograph holder as the basis for a piece of writing.

If you choose not to use working pairs, write a similar set of prompt questions on the board. Give the children ten minutes to think about the answers to each and ask them to choose the most interesting five for their writing.

Point out that the title given to the piece of work can contain information which might not appear in the body of the piece.

4. Packing for a mystery tour

Age range
Seven to nine.

Group size
Pairs.

What you need
Writing materials, destination cards with one of four possible destinations on each card.

What to do
Split the class into working pairs. Tell the children that they are going to go on an imaginary weekend away to a secret destination, which is named on the card you are giving to each pair. The destinations may be realistic or as wild as your imagination allows. Only their partner will know their destination. Space on the tour is limited and they may only take the following:
• twelve items of clothing;
• four items of personal hygiene;
• six personal items of their own choosing.

The children must individually write a list of the things they would take, in order of priority. When they have done this they may compare lists with their partner, but they are not allowed to change anything.

Then explain that, in fact, there are only four mystery tours in the class. The children must try to find others who might be going to the same destination as themselves by displaying their own lists and reading the other children's. They should be encouraged to do this in complete silence and

no one is allowed to tell anyone the name of their own destination.

When the children think that they have found everyone else in the class who is going to the same destination, they should sit together, ready to begin the journey.

Once the class is sitting in four groups you, the teacher, can play the part of the tour operator, checking the tickets. At this point you can choose to take the lesson in one of two different directions.
• You may decide to use this as an opportunity to get the children to discuss the variety or similarity of their choices and the effect they could have on their participation and enjoyment of the holiday.
• Alternatively, you may decide to use this as the start of a drama situation about holidays. What happens when someone suddenly realises that the bus, train, plane, rocket or spaceship on which they are travelling is not going to the right place? What sort of casual conversations do travellers engage in?

5. Writing a postcard

Age range
Seven to nine.

Group size
Individuals.

What you need
Writing materials, card, box.

What to do
This activity is a good one to use at the beginning of term, teaching children how to write their addresses, while encouraging them to consider class members who would not necessarily be drawn to their attention.

Get each child to write his or her address in the accepted way on to a small piece of paper. Put these into a box. Then discuss as a class some of the holidays the children have been on. Try to categorise their destinations by asking:
• Who has been out of the country?
• Who went away in this country?
• Who stayed at home, but did different things from normal?

It is imperative that the children who stayed at home be made to feel the value of their holiday, and you should be able to use your position as questioner to do this during the class discussion.

Ask the children to think about which was the best day of their holiday. Get each child to choose a name and address out of the box, without revealing it to anyone else. The children must then address and write a postcard to the person they picked, telling them about their special day, and illustrating it on the reverse side. Once finished, the postcards should be placed in a special box, to be delivered during the following writing session.

6. Holiday gifts

Age range
Seven to nine.

Group size
Individuals.

What you need
Catalogues, writing materials.

What to do
Give the children catalogues to look at and tell them that they have a certain amount of money to spend – say £50. They must write a list of people for whom they would like to buy a present while on holiday, what they would like to give them, and why. The total cost of the presents must not exceed the stated amount of money.

7. An item from my holiday

Age range
Seven to nine.

Group size
Individuals.

What you need
One item per child, writing materials.

What to do
Ask the children to bring into school one item that reminds them of their holiday. It should not be anything large, nor expensive; for example, a shell from the beach, a piece of wrapping paper or card, a leaf or conker, a sequin, a sweet wrapper or a swimming costume.

Allow the class one minute to silently observe their article. Tell them they are to do some close-observation writing about the object, using one line on their page for each observation, but never actually mentioning the name of the object which they are describing. This should be followed by a description of the event or place that the object reminds them of, mentioning where it was found and why it is special. They may like to write what their thoughts were on seeing the object.

The name of the object should form the title of this piece of writing which is, effectively, about memories of a holiday event. Finally, the children should be encouraged to read all the lines they have written and to delete those which are not absolutely necessary to the feel of the piece.

8. Holiday suitcases

Age range
Seven to nine.

Group size
Whole class.

What you need
Writing materials, a small box for each child and one to hold the name slips.

What to do
This is a good activity to do at the end of the project on holidays or in the week before a school holiday. Each child in the class should make a holiday suitcase, using a small box. These can be hung up in the classroom. Each child must then write his or her name at the top of five pieces of paper and place these in a box.

The names are shaken up and each child must draw out five names. Everybody in the class has to write one good thing about each of the people whose names they have drawn out. The names and comments are then posted into the correct suitcases. Each child will now have a holiday suitcase to take home containing five positive statements about himself or herself.

School

These activities for nine- to twelve-year-olds encourage the children to think about the range of opportunities and options available for them in school, and to reflect on how they currently react to these and why.

1. Memories of school

Age range
Nine to twelve.

Group size
Individuals or pairs.

What you need
Writing materials.

What to do
Put the children into working pairs and allow them five minutes each to tell their partner what they thought school would be like before they came, and how realistic these expectations proved to

be. Emphasise that five minutes is not very long and that it is important that the pairs start talking immediately and do not waste time. If someone can't think of anything to say, her partner may help her to remember by asking questions. You may like to discuss what sort of questions might be helpful before starting the exercise. Warn the class when each side has two minutes and one minute to go.

Ask the children to write individually a short report on their partner's expectations of school. This must be done totally on the basis of what they have just been told and without any further consultation. Only after the reports are finished may they swap and read them. The children should then be allowed 20 minutes in which to add any details which have been omitted or to change experiences which have been represented incorrectly. They should be encouraged to expand upon the experiences already mentioned and to add any others which occur to them, even if these were not

initially mentioned to their partner. Once the reports have been finished, they should be written up in a form that can be shared with the class. Children should be encouraged to comment on how realistic their expectations were and on major areas of disappointment or joy.

2. First weeks of school

Age range
Nine to twelve.

Group size
Pairs, then groups of four.

What you need
Writing materials, space for drama work.

What to do
Give each pair a piece of paper and ask them to divide it into half lengthways, writing 'Good things' at the top of one half and 'Bad things' at the top of the other. Ask the children to list all the good and bad things that happened in the first few weeks of the school year. Plan to allow about 15 minutes for this, but they may require

longer. Then ask the pairs to combine to form groups of four. Allow each pair about ten minutes to explain their list to the other pair in their group, warning them when they are two minutes and one minute from 'time up'.

Tell the groups that they must use this list as the basis for a play about a child's first day at school. The play can be realistic, funny or sad, and the events in it don't have to be true, although they might be based on a true experience. At the end of the session, encourage the groups to show their work to the rest of the class. It is likely that even if the events in the plays are not true, the feelings behind them will be.

Finally, use the opportunity to discuss the children's feelings about coming to school.

Further activity
This work can be developed into a further writing lesson, asking the children to write their plays down, or to produce poetry or personal writing about their feelings. They could also write a letter to the teacher or headteacher telling them how they feel at the start of a new year, the things which have helped them and suggestions for ways in which the experience of entering the school at the beginning of the year could be improved.

3. Why I come to school

Age range
Nine to twelve.

Group size
Individuals.

What you need
Writing materials.

What to do
Introduce the activity by asking the class to brainstorm all that they did the previous day in school. The list should include as wide a range as possible of the social, academic and routine aspects of school life.

Ask the class, working individually, to make two lists; one list of the aspects they enjoy and another of aspects which they think 'improve' them or in some way serve to make them a better person. It may be that the same activity or aspect of school life appears on both lists and that some aspects appear on neither list.

Ask the children to prioritise each list and finally to label each aspect or activity either 'S', for social, 'A', for academic, or 'R', for routine. This will indicate whether they come to school primarily for social, academic or routine reasons. Now the children may compare lists, noting similarities and differences in categories and judgements about activities or aspects of school life.

In groups, the children should be encouraged to question each other about their priorities. It should be made very clear that the lists reflect the personalities and attitudes of the compiler, rather than some qualities inherent in the activities themselves. Thus the basis of the discussion should not be about good or bad aspects of the school, but why particular personalities prefer some aspects to others.

Individuals should use their list to write as honestly as possible about why they come to school, and to signal those aspects which they enjoy and dislike, indicating why this is so in terms of their own personality, attitudes and interests.

Further activity
Ask the class to consider those aspects which appeared in the original brainstorm, but which do not appear on either of their lists. They should label each of these 'essential' or 'non-essential' and say why. Obviously, any activity which is seen as non-essential, not enjoyable and not 'improving' merits further debate.

4. Games we used to play

Age range
Nine to twelve.

Group size
Individuals and the whole class.

What you need
Writing materials.

What to do
For this activity to work well, the class needs to be in a responsive mood. The results will be disappointing if you attempt to do it, for example, after a wet play, on a windy day or when the children are excited about a special event. Use a calm, low, quiet voice to try to introduce an almost hypnotic effect. If any child needs to be told off during the introduction to this lesson, do so silently, without destroying the mood.

Get the class to sit or lie in a comfortable position and to close their eyes. Tell them that they will get an opportunity to talk about their response, but that they must remain silent until you ask them to open their eyes again.

Start by asking the class to remember what they were like when they were five years old. What classroom were they in? Who was their teacher? Who or what did they play with? Each teacher has a different routine for sending the class out to play. What was their routine? What happened when they went out to play? Did they always wait for the same group of friends, or did they join a group once they were outside? Were they always keen to go out, or did they sometimes try to stay inside? Did they have a special part of the playground in which they habitually played? How did they go about joining a game that others were already playing?

Play Time in Primary one

When I was in primary one at play time I sat on my own in a corner of a shelter shivering to keep warm while I watched the other other children play chases and kiss, coudle and torcher and laughing so mutch they had sore stomiehes when they came back into class. I did not have any friends and I was very lonely. Even though I hated having no friends and watching everyone else have a good time I would much rather be out side shivering than inside on wet days because the big girls shouted at everyone. Because of this experience I make a very big effort to find good frends

by Stuart Phifer

Now, without discussing it, ask the class to write about their memories. Tell them that they have only a limited time (about ten minutes) and may write notes if they like. Neatness, handwriting, grammar and spelling do not matter on this occasion.

Next, describe going out to play on a typical cold winter's day in your school. Tell the children to write about how they felt when they were five. What would they have worn on such a day? Can they remember who they played with and how they decided what they would do? Stress that you are interested in how they passed the time during playtimes and you want them to remember everything.

Split the class into two groups and ask each group to do the same for either a rainy or wet playtime or for a very hot summer's day.

Divide the board into three sections headed 'Winter playtimes', 'Wet playtimes' and 'Summer playtimes'. Ask for volunteers to describe their memories, while you listen and record the rough details on the board under the appropriate section. Ask the class if they think current five-year-olds in the school still do the same sort of things as they used to. Tell the class that they are going to write about what they used to do at playtimes and will eventually read this work to the current five-year-olds to see how they respond. They may choose to write about either winter, summer or wet playtimes. They can write about several pastimes or just one particular game they played, but the writing *must* contain lots of detail.

The work should be made into a book, which could be taken and read to the current reception class to see whether times have changed.

5. The trip home from school

Age range
Nine to twelve.

Group size
Individuals.

What you need
Writing and drawing materials.

What to do
Ask the children to think about their journey home from school and to list four landmarks that they regularly see. Beside each landmark, they should write a few lines to describe it and say how they feel each time they see it on their way home. Their feelings, of course, may vary depending on the sort of day they have had.

The trip home from school.

The Co-op supermarket
The BP garage
Lennox Castle Hospital
The farm

At the start of my journey home I pass the BP garage. It is always full with cars. Next main point I think is the Co-op. Thats where we go for small shopping but for big shopping go to asda. We go on a bit further in our journey and we pass Lennox Castle Hospital. This is where a lot of disabled people stay. My friends mum used to work there. Next we pass a white farm house on our right. The farmer who lives there owns a lot of land round Campsie Glen. When I pass here I know I only have a few moments till I get home.
To get to my house you go down a long road surrounded by trees and pass a few houses. My house is a big white house at the end of the village above an arts and craft shop. The time I like coming home best is in cold winter nights. When I see the lights shining from the windows. I know I'm home.

Ask for a volunteer to describe his or her street in detail. For example, in the absence of a street sign, how would they know that they had arrived at the turning for their street, or that they'd arrived at their garden gate or front door? How does it differ from that of their neighbours? Do they have a front garden? If so,

how do they recognise it? It is sometimes harder to do this for towerblocks and flats but, if pressed, children can still tell you details that make the lift, entrance hall or stairs in their tower block different from the other blocks.

Then ask the children to write two paragraphs, one describing the four landmarks they see when they are on their way home and how they feel about them, and the other describing the entrance to their own street, house or flat, paying very close attention to detail. The work should be illustrated with a close-observation drawing, done as homework.

This is an excellent opportunity for you to join the children in their writing, describing your own journey, street and house, but be warned – whatever you write will be avidly read!

These pieces of written work could be made into a book entitled 'Journey home', or displayed on the wall. They look particularly effective when the written work and drawings are supplemented with photographs of the authors on their journey. It is our experience that parents very much enjoy an opportunity to see work such as this, and read it with interest.

6. School uniform

Age range
Nine to twelve.

Group size
Individuals, pairs or small groups.

What you need
Photocopiable page 180 (if required), writing materials, scissors.

What to do
Before doing this activity, choose whether you wish to use the 'for and against school uniform' statements on photocopiable page 180 or whether you would like your class to generate their own ideas. Using the prepared statements gives an instant written vocabulary and structure for children who are slow or lack confidence in writing. It releases them from some of the decisions which make the initial stages of writing slow and laborious, and allows them to focus on the selection and ordering of ideas. However, it may inhibit the free thought of others who would be quite capable of working in groups to conduct their own brainstorm to generate ideas which support or argue against school uniform.

Tell the class that you are interested in their views on school uniform and whether it is a good or bad idea. If the class are using the photocopiable sheet, introduce it and read through the ideas, but do not discuss them at this stage. You may choose to use one sheet per child, or one sheet per pair.

Allow the children time to cut out the statements and sort them into two piles, one 'for' uniform and one 'against'. Then ask the children to rank the ideas in each pile, giving a number one to the most important argument and a five

to the least important. They should do this in secret. Finally, ask the children to share their rankings, and the reasons for them, with the class, emphasising that they are the result of different personal opinions and that there is no one right answer.

Tell the children that they are going to use their ranking to produce a piece of writing about school uniform. They must decide which are the stronger arguments and why. A statement of this decision should be the first thing they write. They may then use the ranked arguments to support it.

They must choose the three highest-ranked arguments which support the opposing point of view, and say why these should not be given so much weight.

When the writing is finished, choose some children to read their work to the rest of the class. Display the work on the board.

Further activity
The children can take home the statements on page 180 and ask their parents to rank them, saying why they chose

that particular order. This can then be written up in the form of a report.

7. What makes a good teacher?

Age range
Nine to twelve.

Group size
Individuals or the whole class.

What you need
Writing materials.

What to do
Talk to the class about what the job of teaching involves and ask them to make a list of the different aspects, while you write their suggestions on the board. Make a clear distinction between what teachers have to do and the personal qualities teachers might need in order to do this. The list will obviously include things like having a wide general knowledge, being able to explain clearly, making learning interesting and enjoyable, being in control, being aware of pastoral and community needs, and so on.

Once this list is on the board, ask the children to choose the five aspects that they feel are the most important and to write them

down in order of priority. If the children are not very quick at copying from the board, it may be helpful to write numbers beside the suggestions on the board and ask the children to simply copy the numbers of those which they think are the most important.

Return to the list on the board and ask the class to suggest the personal qualities they think are needed in order to do each aspect of the job. Again, write these on the board.

Next, tell the children to think about the aspects of teaching which they identified as the most important and use this to identify a prioritised list of personal qualities. Tell them that they are to do a piece of writing entitled 'My ideal teacher', using their list of personal qualities as a basis and justifying their choices by referring to what they consider to be the most important aspects of a teacher's job.

> My Ideal Teacher by Lawrence Turner
>
> My Ideal Teacher would have these 5 things
>
> 1. Helping- willing to help when we need her
> 2. Understanding-this is one of the main things
> 3. A good personality-being able to have a joke every so often.
> 4. Good Ideas- having good ideas to make our work fun.
> 5. Explanations-I would like her to be able to explain things well.
>
> My ideal teacher would be kind and not strict. I would like to be able talk to a teacher at the same level and know that she or he would understand my worries when I told them about them. My godmother is a headmistress in South Africa and she is very different from the English teachers here. When I was there I went on a trip with lots of 4th and 5th year people for four days and two teachers from the same school. It seemed very strange. My ideal teacher would be like one of them. The children called them by their first names and they spoke to each other as though they were sisters or best friends

CHAPTER 8

Poetry writing

In most story writing, personal writing and functional writing, words are used as tools to convey what the author wants to say and to regulate how quickly the storyline unfolds. Although readers appreciate the skill of a writer who is able to do this effectively and efficiently, their main concern is the story itself. The written words are the means whereby the story is uncovered.

Poetry, however, is different. In poetry, the focus is on the power of the words themselves. There are fewer words, and these may be more carefully chosen and arranged by the writer. The rhythm and pattern of a poem further emphasise the linguistic choices the poet has made. They can be seen on the page and heard when the poem is read aloud. This generic economy and selectivity forces each reader to contribute, bridging the gaps by reflecting on the choice of words and interweaving personal memories, feelings and experience with the words of the poem to create the rich tapestry of meanings intended by the poet.

BACKGROUND

Why teach poetry?

Poetry has a very direct appeal. Most people know some poetry by heart, many have a favourite poem and most have, at some point in their lives, tried their hand at writing poetry.

In writing poetry, children learn about economy of expression. They have to make hard choices about words, and through this they learn about language. The economy and brevity of poetry encourage an honest and personal approach to writing, and can often appeal to children who are daunted by writing longer pieces.

The children also learn about the role of the reader; they know that poetry must harness and utilise the reader's imagination in order to work its magic. It is possible to teach specific techniques to help do this, but these are not enough; to write poetry well, the child must learn how to use such techniques effectively. This empathy can only be developed through responding as a reader to the poetry of others.

In short, through writing poetry, children learn about the craft of using language not only to express but to arouse the full spectrum of human emotions, from humour to fear and from sorrow to joy.

How to teach poetry

In many ways, teaching poetry presents the same problems as teaching personal writing; the teacher must choose a thought-provoking stimulus and structure the lesson to allow space and time for individual responses. Yet a poetry lesson demands more than this, for it must also focus the child's attention sharply on the subtleties of language and meaning; how the choice and juxtaposition of words or ideas can create different layers of meaning, prompting different levels of response in the reader. This can only be done through discussion and reflection. Of course, a good poetry teacher introduces children to simple poetic techniques, but she also recognises that these, in themselves, are useless without plenty of opportunities to discuss and practise applying them.

ACTIVITIES

1. List poems

Age range
Six to eight.

Group size
Individuals and the whole class.

What you need
Writing materials, beautiful pictures and posters of scenery.

What to do
Children should be made aware of the distinction between story and poetry writing, and discussion of the conventions and structure of a list poem are often a good starting point for this. Obviously, the teacher is the best judge of when an individual child or class is ready for such work.

List poems have a very simple structure that children grasp easily. They depend on the basic principle that each new idea is written on a new line. The simplicity of this structure allows both the teacher and children to concentrate on the language of poetry.

Display a picture near the chalkboard and ask the children to give one idea at a time about the picture. Write these, one under the other, as a list on the chalkboard, beginning each new idea on a new line with a capital letter. When you have five or six ideas, ask the class to read them through and decide, if this was handed in as a piece of written work, what type of writing it would be. They will probably recognise it as a poem (of sorts). Explain that poems rely on far fewer explanation or linking words than stories do. Discuss which words are really important to keep the sense and mood of the poem, and which can be discarded. Those words which evoke pictures, feelings and memories are essential. With the class, go through the poem on the board, rubbing out redundant words and perhaps rephrasing some lines so that the words that are left make sense.

Finally, give each child or group a picture to write poetry about. We have found that this activity works very well with pictures of the seasons. The final work can be made into beautiful class calendars with a picture, a verse and the days for each month.

2. What am I?

Age range
Six to eight.

Group size
Individuals and the whole class.

What you need
Drawing and writing materials.

What to do
Tell the children to imagine that they are some inanimate object. Tell them that they must describe themselves in a list poem, with each new idea beginning on a new line. Only the last line may mention what, in fact, they are. To help the children structure their work, write the following plan on the chalkboard:
• What colour are you? ('I am...')
• What shape are you?
• What size are you?
• How old are you?
• Where can you be found?
• What sounds can you make?
• Who are your friends and neighbours?
• Who is your worst enemy?
• What do you wish?
• What are you?

Show the children a sample poem on the chalkboard using this structure. Cover the last line and let the children guess what or who the poem is

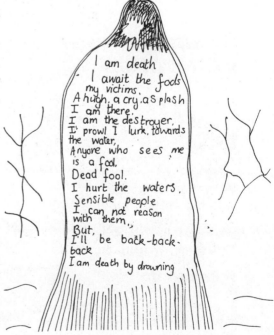

I am death
I await the fools
my victims.
A hush, a cry, as plash
I am there.
I am the destroyer,
I prowl I lurk, towards
the water,
Anyone who sees me
is a fool,
Dead fool.
I hurt the waters,
Sensible people
I can not reason
with them,
But, I'll be back-back-
back
I am death by drowning

about. Then suggest that the children write their own poems, making sure that no one knows what they have chosen for the subject. Remind them that carefully thought out language will make their work a poem rather than just a guessing game. Ask them to try to express the very essence of the object in their writing. Once finished, poems should be read and displayed in the classroom, or as part of a class book of 'Who am I?' poems.

Further activity
To give the reader an added clue, the children could write their poem in the shape of the object it describes.

3. Simple alliteration

Age range
Six to eight.

Group size
Pairs.

What you need
Suitable alliterative poems such as 'Silver' by Walter de la Mare or 'The Eagle' by Tennyson, writing materials.

What to do
It is important that children understand and experience the satisfaction of reading poetry aloud. One technique that even young children quickly recognise is alliteration, and they take enormous pleasure in reciting alliterative poems. Once children have become aware of the technique, they are keen to try it themselves. This makes an excellent language activity because it doesn't involve an enormous amount of writing, but it does involve a lot of thinking about words, how they sound and what they mean.

At this age, it is probably best to let the children experience the technique through reading and writing poetry, leaving complicated explanations until they are older.

Begin by writing a few concrete nouns on the chalkboard. Animals are always good starting points; 'tiger', 'slug', 'rabbit' and so on. Ask the children to work with a partner and to try to think of one word to describe, for example, the tiger, beginning with the same initial sound. Take various suggestions from the class and write them on the chalkboard. Tell the children to choose one (or two!) and to copy the phrase on to their own piece of paper. Then tell the children to finish the line by describing something the tiger is doing; it can be something sensible or something silly, but most of the words must begin with the letter 't'.

Collect examples of the sentences the children have written and copy them on to the chalkboard for others to see and discuss.

Give each pair a different word to try on their own. Vary the type of words and the type of sounds, offering some 'hard' sounds and some 'softer' ones such as 'rain' or 'shell'. Older children can be given more abstract words, like 'blizzard', 'mountain' or 'feather'.

4. Sense poems

Age range
Six to nine.

Group size
Individuals.

What you need
Writing materials.

What to do
A sense poem provides a simple structure within which children can explore ideas about almost any subject; spring, the sea, the forest, a tramp, a holiday, and so on. The structure is basic, with each line starting with one of the senses and describing how the subject of the poem affects the writer in this respect. For example, a poem about 'The sea' might read:
'I *see*... waves crashing on the shore.
I *hear*... the call of the gulls.
I *smell*... salt and seaweed blowing on the wind.
I *touch*... cool, smooth pebbles, ice cold water.
I *feel*... excited, happy and a little afraid.'
The 'I feel' part of the poem can describe something that is actually touched with the fingers, or an emotion.

It is a good idea to take ideas from the children and use them to build up a class poem on the board first of all. This illustrates the structure and method, and shows that it is important to think aloud, sort through suggestions, consider possibilities, experiment and discard initial ideas when composing poetry.

Children may choose to leave the line starter in their poem or to omit it. Omitting the line starter can make the poem much more evocative and effective, but may mean reorganising the words. One nine-year-old, Catherine, changed the above poem to:

'Waves crashing on the shore
The wild call of gulls wheeling
   in the sky
The strong smell of seaweed
   blows on the wind
Icy salted water crashes on my
   legs
The sea makes me a little
   afraid.'

5. Colour poems

Age range
Six to nine.

Group size
Individuals and the whole class.

What you need
Writing materials.

What to do
Ask the children what thoughts spring to mind when they consider certain colours. It is usually best to focus on one colour in class discussion. Young children will probably suggest very simple, concrete associations, but older ones should be encouraged to suggest more abstract ideas.

Each line of the poem should repeat the name of the colour. For example: 'Red is anger/ Red is the way I feel when my bike finally reaches the top of the hill...'.

It is important to make it clear to older children that one-word lines, while sometimes acceptable, might be improved with a short phrase of explanation, for example: 'Red is the blood that stained the grass when I fell...'

After composing a whole-class poem, allow the children to choose their own colour to write about. The best may be that which conjures up the most images in a brainstorm. Once finished, children may drop the 'Red is...' starter line and freely refashion their own lines, only occasionally using the colour word.

6. You are...

Age range
Six to nine.

Group size
Individuals.

What you need
An interesting subject about which the children are fairly knowledgeable, perhaps from a topic; writing materials.

What to do
One way to encourage children to feel empathy with others is to introduce them to the idea of writing a poem which speaks *to* its subject. The immediacy and simplicity of this convention often produces very appealing results.

Explain that each line of the poem begins 'You are...'. The poet must finish the line by describing how he feels about

the subject and what he most admires about it.

Once again, the child may choose to drop some or all of the starter phrases after the initial ideas have been generated and the first rough draft is complete. One child, Neil, wrote a poem called 'Icarus'.

'Your wings allow you to glide
   and soar,
The sun is very close,
It is pulling you up like a
   magnet,
The sensation of freedom
   pulses inside you and the
   feeling wipes your memory
   clean.
Up, up, up you go, up towards
   the sun,
Icarus, Icarus you're going too
   high
If you go any higher the wax
   will melt,
It's too late...
The sun is too close,
The feathers are spinning
   down to earth,
Suddenly you start to fall,
The sea is now your fate.'

7. Spells

Age range
Seven to nine.

Group size
Individuals, pairs or the whole class.

What you need
Writing materials, alphabet clearly displayed.

What to do
Explain to the children that a spell is more than a list of horrible ingredients mixed together to make magic. Reciting the spell is like adding another ingredient; the words must be spoken, or the magic

won't work. Spells are always written in rhyme, since this makes them easier to remember.

Ask the class to suggest one horrible thing to put into the cauldron and start the spell off. Write this as an alliterative sentence on the board; for example, 'A dead dog's eye'. This then becomes the first line of the spell.

Taking the last word of the first line, show the children how to find rhyming words by going through the letters of the alphabet and replacing the initial letter of the chosen word to make a series of new words. Ask the children to suggest a second line which might end in one of these words and therefore rhyme with the first line. Select one of their suggestions to write down.

Then ask the children to suggest another ingredient. This will be the beginning of a new rhyme, and so it should

not rhyme with the first two lines.

Repeat the above process to create another rhyming couplet. For younger classes, the spell may end with the third rhyming couplet, leaving the title to explain the spell's purpose. Older children, however, should be encouraged to add a fourth couplet which rounds the spell off and explains the action of the magic; for example: 'Stir this around a time or two/ To make my brother lose his shoe'.

8. Compiling an anthology

Age range
Seven to twelve.

Group size
Individuals.

What you need
Writing materials.

What to do
Explain that an anthology is a collection of poetry written by many different poets. Often we find a poem that we like very

much, but unless we learn it by heart, we forget where we read it. It is therefore a good idea to copy out poems that we like and keep them all together in one book.

Explain that each individual in the class is going to compile an anthology of favourite poems. They can write some of the poems themselves, some can come from other books, and others can be written by their classmates.

Children love the idea of having free choice as to what they copy into their personal anthologies, since so much of what they read and do in school is prescribed, so let them take their anthologies home with them or to the library.

It is important to show interest and enthusiasm for children's anthologies, and it is good to be seen compiling one yourself. How exciting for the children if the teacher chooses to include one of their poems in his or her anthology. Of course, it is essential to include one poem from each pupil over the course of the year.

It is also a valuable exercise to put some time aside every few weeks for a swapping session to share good poetry found recently. Encourage the children to decorate their favourite poems or illustrate them, and ask them to record where they found each poem and the date on which they found it.

Another idea is to encourage the children to ask their friends and relations to copy a poem into their anthology. Alternatively, the children could scribe for their parents.

9. Impossible dreams

Age range
Seven to twelve.

Group size
Individuals and the whole class.

What you need
Writing materials, *Sky in the Pie* by Roger McGough (Puffin).

What to do
Begin this activity with an exercise to encourage the children to think in an abstract way. With older children, you may choose to precede the lesson by reading Roger McGough's poem 'Sky in the Pie' from his anthology of the same name. Younger children will benefit from an introductory activity which stimulates thought about the vocabulary of whichever sense is to be considered; for example, you could introduce a 'feely box' or a tasting, smelling or listening activity.

Then seat the class in a circle on the floor. You may choose to explain that you eventually want them to write an 'impossible dream' response poem, attributing new sensory dimensions to familiar objects, colours or emotions in a way that is only possible in a dream, or you may choose to introduce the exercises as simply a game, only explaining about the dream when it comes to writing individual poems.

Begin with some very easy rounds. For example:
• 'If I could hear the playground it would...';
• 'If I could hear my pencil it would...';
• 'If I could hear the sun it would...'.

Ask each child in the circle to contribute an ending. Encourage originality by writing the best endings on a large sheet of paper at the end of each round.

Once the children have gained in confidence, try asking for more abstract responses *either* by changing to a more abstract sensory mode *or* by using a more abstract type of stimulus.

Be careful not to suddenly make it very abstract at this stage, or it will throw the class. We have found that sound and touch are the easiest senses to start with, and smell is the most difficult. You might say: 'Green sounds like...' or 'Fear sounds like...'. Or you might say: 'The sun smells like...'.

After four or five rounds, ask the children to return to their seats with the writing materials. Give them a list of about twelve objects, emotions or colours and ask them to choose three or four from it to form the basis of their individual poems. They could start the poem with: 'In my dream...'.

Amy Blount

In my dreams
I could hear
the stars saying
lets be brighter
than the moon tonight

I could hear
A rock saying
I want to
Eat a big bowl
of Soup I'm cold
from the Sea

In my dreams
I could hear
the Word Book say
I want Some more
words

10. Similes

Age range
Eight to twelve.

Group size
Individuals and the whole class.

What you need
Writing materials.

What to do
For the younger children it is enough if they know that a simile describes something that looks or is like the subject of the poem. Older children can be introduced to the more sophisticated idea that a really successful and striking simile often compares things which are very different, apart from one element. It is this that produces freshness and surprise, focusing the reader's attention very directly on the one similarity.

These poems can follow the basic structure of a list poem.

Begin by giving the children a heading, for example 'The witch'. Explain that the poem they should try to write will tell the reader exactly what the essence of a witch is, without actually mentioning that this is what it is about. Each line of the poem should begin with or contain the word 'Like' and will explain exactly what the witch looks like.

Write suggestions on the board in the form of a list poem (see Activity 1 on page 109). As this exercise continues, some children will begin to think in increasingly abstract terms, and this will help others also to think in this way. Then write another list, this time asking for similes to describe what the witch sounds like.

Finally, go through the process of tidying the language and ideas on the chalkboard, getting the children to suggest what should be deleted or altered.

When the language is sorted out, the position of lines within the poem should be considered and altered if necessary. This can be done with children working on the poem as a class, individually or in pairs, eventually comparing their results as a class.

After the children have gone through this process for a class poem, they will feel more confident to try writing their own. You can either give them the same subject as for the class poem, or a similar one. Tell the children to try to use their own ideas, but if they get stuck, to borrow from the class poem. This gives all the children a safety net of ideas, as well as room to expand their own thoughts.

Children can write simile poems about a whole host of different subjects, using the method described above. It is useful and interesting to point out the use of similes in poetry you read to the class, and to encourage the children to recognise them. It is, of course, a technique which can also be transferred to prose writing.

11. Writing a song

Age range
Eight to twelve.

Group size
Pairs.

What you need
A tape of a suitable tune, a tape recorder, writing materials.

What to do
It is best to base this activity on a tune which is fairly simple and either has no words or has words with which the children are unfamiliar.

Play the tape to the class several times, until they know it very well. Then tell the class that they are going to work in pairs to write words to fit this tune.

Each pair should decide what their song will be about.

To help them do this, ask them individually to list three possible topics and then discuss with their partner which offers the most possibilities.

The children will probably decide to compose the words together, choosing words, rhymes and phrases which fit the structure and rhythm of the tune. Emphasise that they will improve as they get towards the end of the song, and then they may want to rethink the phrasing of earlier lines.

Some children will be helped if they have an opportunity to listen to the tune at certain points during the composing period. Others, however, will simply find this distracting. It is best, therefore, either to play the tape at intervals or to arrange for those children who want to refresh their memories to have access to the tape, where it will not disturb others.

Once the children have decided on their words they should copy them in their best handwriting. The pairs can then perform their songs in front of the rest of the class. The children can also be encouraged to choose a famous singer whom they would like to record their song.

Further activities

• Suggest that the children organise a class pop concert, with each pair writing and performing their own song, written especially for the occasion.

• The children can use the same technique to write their own 'rap'. Make sure that you first establish a basic pattern for this sort of song by playing some suitable examples to the class.

12. Movement poems

Age range
Eight to twelve.

Group size
Groups of three or four, and the whole class.

What you need
Writing materials, photocopiable page 181.

What to do
Ask the children to imagine the journey of a small stream flowing through the grass to a waterfall plunging down on to rocks, eventually trickling into a large, calm lake. Show the picture of the stream's journey on photocopiable page 181, and explain that they are going to write a poem about the stream, remembering that poetry is all about the sound and meaning of words.

Elicit from the children the type of mood that each part of the stream's journey evokes and get them to brainstorm words which might be associated with each mood.

Show them how the words could be arranged on the page and written in a style and manner which also evokes the general mood the children are trying to portray. For example, the waterfall words could be in bold, large, dynamic capitals, and arranged as though falling down in straight lines, like a waterfall. Words describing the lake will be calm, even and smooth, arranged to glide and swirl round in a circular motion, portraying the peaceful, gentle motion of the water at this stage. Those which describe how the water seeps from the rocks into the

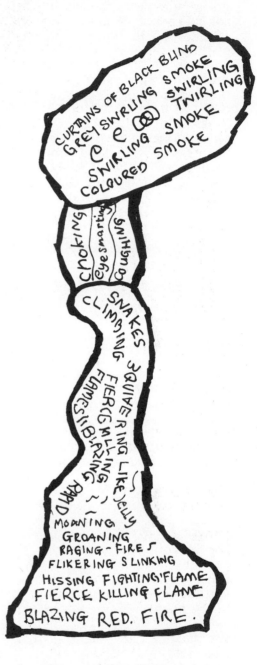

lake will be written differently again, as will the words describing the stream as it meanders through the pastures before becoming a waterfall. Show the class how to do this for *one* part of the stream's journey.

It is possible to make a group poem with this activity, asking each child in a group to take responsibility for one part of the stream's journey. The children should write rough drafts of ideas first, and then discuss how best to collate these with the parts done by other group members, copying out the final, agreed version.

Fire is another good subject for this sort of poem. It should start with the burning wood, and go on to the red-hot centre, the flames and finally the swirling smoke rising above.

13. In someone else's shoes

Age range
Eight to twelve.

Group size
Individuals and the whole class.

What you need
Writing materials.

The Pit From The Trappers Point Of View
by James Friel

I sat in my hole just like a mouse
Almost dropping dead with fatigue
My rope was swaying with the
                                shadows
As if they had just come alive

    shivered with cold and also
                        with fear
And I heard a frightening sound
A girl was pulling a trolley of coal
She collapsed and dreamed of bed

A girl with a waist all red with
                            blood
Was drugged by a dying boy
The chain and the tir
                had killed her for sure

Or else she had choaked on
                        sweat

I bumped my head up on a rock
to keep myself awake
In here, asleep meant dead.

What to do
This activity asks the children to imagine what it is like to be someone or something else. It is a good idea to start by using creatures or objects which are restricted or lack freedom in a way with which the children are familiar; for example, a scarecrow. Elicit from the children what it must be like to be a scarecrow, always to be dressed in ragged clothes, not to be able to move and to have the job of scaring others away. Encourage the idea that some may be saddened by this life, whereas others may enjoy it. When you have built up a feeling of empathy in the class, ask them to imagine that they are the scarecrow and to write a list poem telling others about themselves and how they feel. This type of poetry can become very sad, angry or indignant.

Further activity
Children respond well to writing this type of poetry if they are given a picture to examine. The concrete images stimulate ideas and sometimes quite passionate emotions, particularly with subjects such as 'The clown' or 'The witch'.

14. Tie-dye poems

Age range
Eight to twelve.

Group size
Individuals and pairs.

What you need
Squares of white cotton, cold water dye, stones, string, buckets or containers, iron and ironing board, coloured paper, writing materials.

What to do
Children's own work can be a wonderful stimulus for all types of writing. Tie-dye pictures made by the children can be a very interesting stimulus for poetry.

First, get the class to tie-dye white squares in various colours and iron and mount the results on complementary backing paper. Then ask the children to look closely at the patterns they have created and jot down any ideas or images that spring to mind. Ask the children to remember what it was like when they put the white material into the bucket of dye, and to write about this. Again, once the rough ideas have been recorded, give the children time to reword them into a poem.

15. Alliterative alphabet

Age range
Nine to twelve.

Group size
Pairs and the whole class.

What you need
Writing materials.

What to do
It is important that children understand that poetry is usually written to be read aloud and that the sounds and rhythms of the words contribute to the overall effect on the reader. Alliteration is a technique used by poets to emphasise and draw attention to the rhythm and quality of the language by choosing words which all begin with the same initial sound.

Before this activity, read and discuss with the class a

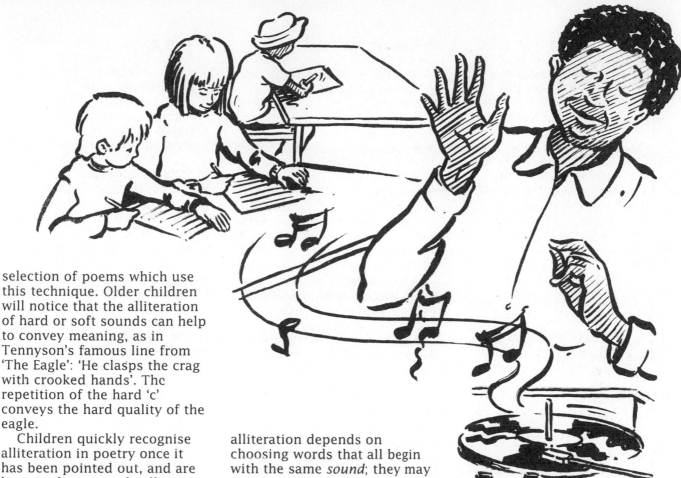

selection of poems which use this technique. Older children will notice that the alliteration of hard or soft sounds can help to convey meaning, as in Tennyson's famous line from 'The Eagle': 'He clasps the crag with crooked hands'. The repetition of the hard 'c' conveys the hard quality of the eagle.

Children quickly recognise alliteration in poetry once it has been pointed out, and are keen to discuss and collect examples from their own reading for a class display. Many will begin to use this technique themselves, simply because they have become aware of it. However, some may welcome an opportunity for more specific practice.

Having explained and discussed examples of alliteration, divide the class into pairs. Explain that, as a bit of fun rather than a serious poetry lesson, the class is going to make 'an alliterative alphabet'. Each pair of children will be responsible for *three* letters of the alphabet and they must invent one alliterative sentence for each letter.

At this point you will probably need to remind the children that letters have *names* and *sounds*, and that

alliteration depends on choosing words that all begin with the same *sound*; they may or may not have the same initial letter. It is also worth emphasising that unusual and exotic words make the most exciting and interesting sentences to read; the children would be well advised to consult their dictionaries!

When allocating letters to the pairs, try to give each pair some easy sounds and one harder sound to work with. Bear in mind also the children's language ability, and give the really hard sounds to those who will cope with them best. Obviously, some letters will be given to more than one group of children and will therefore be used to generate several alliterative sentences. The children should be encouraged to read and discuss the work produced by other pairs in the class.

16. Free poetry

Age range
Nine to twelve.

Group size
Individuals.

What you need
Prepared tapes, writing materials.

What to do
Dramatic music can stimulate ideas by expressing a mood. Play some music to the children and ask them to jot down a list of ideas or thoughts that occur to them

while listening to the music. Use a very short snatch of music, carefully chosen for dramatic effect. When the children have noted their ideas they can sort them, keeping the strongest. They can then reorganise them into the format of one thought per line.

Stress to the children that their poem can be disjointed, or it can express thoughts about a particular theme. It is their choice, and will probably depend on the nature and diversity of their original ideas.

17. Haiku

Age range
Nine to twelve.

Group size
Individuals and the whole class.

What you need
Writing materials.

What to do
Explain to the children that words break up into syllables. A syllable is part of a word

which contains one vowel sound.

Give the children some examples of words and, together, clap the rhythm of syllables in the words. Allow the children to have plenty of practice with this, clapping and stressing the syllables in their own names and in the names of the other children in the class.

When you feel that the class can really hear the syllables and understand what they are, explain to them that there is a Japanese type of poetry called *haiku*. In this type of poem, only 17 syllables may be used. Each new idea begins on a new line and usually the poems have three or four lines, although some have more and some have less.

Choose any theme that is 'current' in the classroom or school and use the chalkboard to demonstrate this type of poetry. Ask the children to give you one line of poetry on this theme, for example: 'Sun slips below the horizon.'

Count the number of syllables used. In this case it is eight, which leaves nine syllables still to be used. Ask for a second line; for example: 'Darkness has fallen.'

This line has five syllables, leaving only four for the final line. Ask the children to suggest a final line with four syllables, for example: 'Night is secret.'

Organising the lines to fit the number of syllables often involves a great deal of crossing out and reorganising. The children may find that they need to alter earlier lines in order to arrive at a poem of just 17 syllables. The results of the exercise, however, are simple and often extremely effective.

18. Fear!

Age range
Nine to twelve.

Group size
Individuals.

What you need
Writing materials.

What to do
Ask the children to imagine what fear would look like if it was a person. They may suggest that it would resemble things of which they are afraid.

Ask them to write a list poem as if Fear were speaking to the reader. What would it say? How would it describe itself? For example:
'I am tall and thin
Covered in a black cloak
Wherever people are alone
  in the night
I am there...'
Ask the children not to say who is speaking until the last line. Talk about how they can gradually build up suspense.

This activity works equally well with other abstract ideas such as 'love' and 'happiness'.

19. Festival of poetry

Age range
Nine to twelve.

Group size
Individuals, groups of six and the whole class.

What you need
Writing materials.

What to do
This activity will require several sessions plus one whole day in the middle of the

Winter

Trees are whistling and bare
Grass is white now
Owls hunt
All the swans are gone

By Steven Craven

Poetry festival

school year. The activity raises the profile of poetry in the classroom by harnessing the general community interest in poetry. Poetry already written by the class may be used, and the 'festival day' serves to provide a new thrust of interest in poetry for the second half of the year.

Children need to be prepared for this day and to play some part in organising it themselves in order for it to be really successful and grab the imagination of the class. It is a good idea to begin some of the preparations for the festival day at least one month in advance.
• Decide on a date.
• Discuss the idea with the children and have a class brainstorm about what might happen during the festival day.
• Make a plan of action based on this brainstorm, and display it in the classroom.

Try to make particular individuals or groups of children responsible for specific tasks. Some of the ideas that might be suggested are as follows.
• Write to famous people or local dignitaries, asking for their favourite poem.
• Write to a local poet asking him or her to come and read a poem on the day.
• List local people or businesses, theatre groups, libraries, secondary schools, bookshops or clubs who may be able to help.
• Collect one favourite poem from each teacher, classroom helper, lunch-time supervisor,

caretaker and so on, and display them.
• Ask each parent to send in a poem they have written, or a favourite poem, along with a short note saying why they wrote or like it.
• Ask the children to teach their parents, school governors or groups from other classes to write a particular type of poetry.

About two weeks before the festival day, split the children into groups of about six. Each group must decide on a presentation they would like to give on the day. It can be about any aspect of poetry they like. You could give them some ideas:
• group poetry speaking;
• illustrations of a poem, which could be shown while it is being recited;
• a narrative poem acted out;
• a shadow puppet show to illustrate a poem.

The group presentation should end with each child choosing and reading the best poem they have written that year.

Any of the ideas suggested in this chapter may be used in order to encourage children to write poetry. The festival presentations can be organised as a single unit, or they can be

timetabled, with each group doing theirs perhaps three times in different areas of the school.

Between presentations, the children could sell refreshments, distribute programmes or entertain visiting dignitaries by giving conducted tours of the poetry displays which have been mounted for the festival. (Remember to leave room on display boards for visitors who have not already contributed a poem to write up their own favourite.)

Plan to have a grand finish to the poetry day; for example:
• a speech about poetry by a local dignitary;
• a theatre group presentation;
• a performance by school staff.

After the festival day, it is essential to set aside some time for the children to evaluate the success of the day. Ask them to consider what aspects must be improved for the next time, and to write letters of thanks to all those who took part and helped make the day a success.

CHAPTER 9

Conventions of writing

The conventions of writing are the universally accepted customs of punctuation, grammar and lexis. They are of central importance for written language because they enable the writer to communicate clearly and unambiguously. They are called the 'surface features' of writing, as they are immediately seen and easily judged. This also adds to their importance, because many readers make judgements about the surface features before assessing more abstract aspects to do with the quality of ideas and their organisation and expression. It is a sad fact of life that the former judgements will often affect the latter; untidy handwriting, poor spelling or ambiguous grammar can detract from the reader's understanding of the author's intentions and reduce the motivation to read on; it becomes too much like hard work!

Ideally, all writing should make the reader think 'This looks good, the ideas make sense, let's read on'.

BACKGROUND

How should we teach the conventions?

There is one basic principle which underlies all success or failure in teaching children to use the conventions correctly. This is that children will learn if they are encouraged to see the sense behind the convention, and to understand how it can help them to communicate more clearly.

This assumes that the child views writing as a purposeful, valid act of communication in the first place. Children who lack an understanding of the needs of their readers, or who have no real desire to express themselves in their written work, will see no point in learning or remembering how to use the conventions.

Clearly, teaching the conventions cannot be separated from their use in actual written communication.

Problems of teaching the conventions

Because the conventions of writing are most effectively learned when children need to use them in 'real' writing, the acquisition of spelling, punctuation and grammar rules is not hierarchical in any absolute sense. Many children grasp points of punctuation or spelling patterns in an order different from that laid down in published schemes, using them unerringly, simply because they have 'noticed' them in their reading or in the work of other, often older children.

This however, creates problems of planning and class organisation for the teacher. Not all children in the class will experience the need at the same time and it is impossible to predict, let alone plan, when this need will arise in individuals or groups. Observation shows that good teachers use a variety of teaching and planning strategies in order to present structured teaching about particular conventions at a time when the children will find it most relevant.

One strategy is to create a need by planning situations and tasks which require the use of particular conventions,

Writing book
John James
Class 4

timetabling the necessary teaching input to answer that need. Thus, an experienced teacher will foresee that children writing a sketch for the school assembly will benefit from a clear explanation of the conventions for writing dialogue, and provide this in a planned and structured session.

Another strategy is to monitor closely the work of the class, noting when a significant number of children require reminding or teaching about a particular rule. This is then swiftly revised with a mini-lesson to the whole class. After this, all the children can be asked to use the convention in their writing and to look at their previous work and identify whether they really understand or need to consider the convention more closely. If so, they should present themselves to the teacher, who can give further help.

Much successful teaching is done when teachers observe individual children working and assess their work. This often involves sensitive decisions about when to interrupt the progression of ideas with a 'writing

conference' to introduce or remind the child about a convention.

Writing conferences are regular, short interviews in which teachers discuss work with individual children. It must be emphasised that they are not solely, or even mainly, to teach the conventions; all aspects of the writing process should be discussed. Ideally, these sessions should be used to listen to the child explaining and expressing his thoughts and to discuss with the child how problems might be overcome. Writing conferences are ideal times to discuss the writing conventions, however, because the teacher is cast primarily in the role of listener. As such, her job is to look for the sense behind the errors; why is a convention ignored or misapplied, why is a spelling pattern consistently wrong?

Wrong practice clearly results from poor or misguided understanding. Therefore, to change wrong practice, it is necessary to challenge and change the understanding which underlies it.

Empowering children through knowledge

It is clear that children who learn the conventions in this way work from what they already know and understand through to a new level of knowledge and understanding. This is empowering for both teachers and children. The question is no longer 'What don't you know?' or 'What mistakes do you make?', but 'What current understanding do you have?'.

The learning of language is a dynamic process and awareness precedes use. By examining the function of the conventions from the standpoint of knowledge gained through years of experience in reading and writing, children may come to see the conventions as useful tools for communication, rather than rods with which they are regularly beaten.

ACTIVITIES

1. Handwriting: forming letters

Age range
Five to six.

Group size
Individuals.

What you need
Templates of lower-case letters, card, corrugated card, sand, adhesive, scissors, marker pens, writing materials.

What to do
Young children can be taught handwriting conventions in conjunction with early phonic awareness. Lessons should focus on one letter at a time, teaching its name, the sound it makes and how it is written. Letters with the same starting point and the same basic hand movement should be taught in succession; for example, a, c, d, g, o and q, or n and m.

Letter formation should be taught using a wide variety of contexts and materials; chalkboards, paint, wet and dry sand, fat crayons, felt-tipped pens and so on.

Show the children how to draw around the templates on to the card, making sure that they have the template the right side up. Then, help them to cut it out. Using the spreader like a pencil, the children should spread adhesive over their letter and sprinkle sand on to it. Finally, after shaking the excess sand off, they should use a bright-coloured pen to indicate the starting point, should anyone want to trace over the letter. Textured letters can also be made from corrugated card.

Once finished, the letters can be mounted and displayed. Children should be encouraged to trace their own and other children's letters, inviting friends to watch and see if they are doing it correctly. They can trace the letter shapes with their eyes open and try again with them closed.

2. Raising phonic awareness

Age range
Five to six.

Group size
Individuals.

What you need
Writing materials.

What to do
While scribing for a child, discuss what letters you will write to begin particular words. Encourage the child to identify the initial sound of the word before you write it.

This 'incidental' learning about phonics also conveys an important message about spelling and writing to the child: that words, sounds and letters are related. You are modelling an important strategy which the child will remember in the future when he or she is 'stuck' for a spelling.

3. When is handwriting important?

Age range
Five to twelve.

Group size
Pairs or groups of eight.

What you need
Photocopiable page 182, blank cards, writing materials, Blu-Tack.

What to do
Ask the children to cut out all the statements on photocopiable page 182. They should work in pairs to consider the statements carefully and prioritise them, placing the situation in which they consider handwriting to be the most important at the top of their blank card and that in which they consider it to be least important at the bottom. The other situations should be slotted in between in order of priority.

The pairs should join together to form groups of eight. One child in each group should then be elected chairperson, and the pairs can share their opinions, arriving at a final agreed order of priority.

Finally, and most importantly, ask one child from each group (not the chairperson) to report to the rest of the class on the debate and the final group decisions.

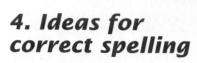

4. Ideas for correct spelling

Age range
Seven to twelve.

Group size
Individuals, pairs and groups of four.

What you need
Poster paper, felt-tipped pens.

What to do
Talk to the children about what they do when they don't know how to spell a word. Ask them each to write down two ideas for how they could find a correct spelling.

In pairs, the children should put their ideas together, and then join into groups of four before writing a final group list of ideas. These should then be collated into a single class list and displayed in the classroom.

Although the final list will obviously depend on the resources in the classroom, it will almost certainly include such ideas as:
• using a dictionary;
• checking with a friend;
• 'trying' the word in different ways on rough paper to see which looks right;
• guessing;
• sounding it out;
• trying to think of a rhyming word which they can spell;
• trying to remember whether they have read the word recently and if so, when and where.

5. Examining punctuation

Age range
Seven to twelve.

Group size
Groups of four to five.

What you need
OHP transparencies and pens or large sheets of paper and marker pens.

What to do
Ask the children to individually write down all the punctuation marks they know how to use, and to share these with the rest of the group, compiling a group list. Then ask each group member to choose three punctuation marks from the list and to write when, how and why they are used, giving one good example of each type.

Each item on the list should then be considered in turn. The group must arrive at a common definition to explain how each punctuation mark should be used, and a scribe should write the explanation beside the mark to which it refers.

Further activity
The children should write a list of all the punctuation marks they have seen, but do not personally use because they are unsure about them. They may need to refer to books in order to identify the different sorts of punctuation.

The exercise serves to raise awareness of punctuation and to provide an agenda for future discussions and teaching.

6. Using capital letters

Age range
Seven to twelve.

Group size
Individuals or groups of four to five.

What you need
Writing materials.

What to do
Ask the children individually to list all the occasions on which they know they should use

capital letters. Allow about five minutes for compiling this list, and warn the children when they have one minute left. At the end of the allotted time, ask each child to read his or her list to the group.

Tell the groups to use these contributions to draw up a set of rules for the use of capital letters. Once each rule has been finalised and agreed by the group, it should be written on to a large poster to be displayed in the writers' corner.

Each child in the group should contribute one example of a sentence which illustrates each rule.

Further activity

Another interesting and enjoyable way of focusing on capital letters is to look at examples of illuminated first letters. Children enjoy illuminating their own letters and may like to copy out a psalm, riddle or poem, illuminating the first letter.

This is a good way to explore how capitalisation, handwriting and presentation overlap.

7. Language questionnaire

Age range
Eight to twelve.

Group size
Individuals and pairs.

What you need
Photocopiable page 183, writing materials.

What to do
To place language at the centre of the curriculum and raise children's awareness of the conventions, it is a good idea to search out children's ideas and impressions of what language work is about.

The questionnaire on photocopiable page 183 provides a way for the children to express their views of the activities and ideas which surround them from the moment they step into school. Knowing what the children think gives a starting point for teaching, and provides a baseline against which progress can be measured.

Explain to the class that you are interested in their views of

language work. Ask the class to work in pairs, and tell them that you want to know their personal points of view, so they should say exactly what they think, not what they think you want them to say. Stress that there are no 'correct' answers, only opinions. The 'right' responses are those which reflect the children's opinions. You will not be marking the questionnaires, so you do not mind if children do not put their names on them.

Although the children are working in pairs, they will each have their own questionnaire. After discussing each question, they should write their own opinions. It does not matter if the pairs disagree.

8. Spelling partners

Age range
Eight to twelve.

Group size
Individuals and pairs.

What you need
Exercise books, writing materials.

What to do
Learning lists of spellings is only worthwhile if the children are learning words which they

know they use and have problems spelling.

For this activity, children need a regular spelling partner with whom they can learn to work well, since the method outlined here places responsibility for learning spellings very much on the shoulders of the individual child.

On a particular day of each week the pairs of children should look back through their past week's writing. With the help of his partner, each child should select six to eight words with which he has had difficulty. The problematic words should then be written in a list on a page in the exercise book.

The next day the children should spend some time studying the 'hard spots' of their chosen words. The following study method should be taught to the children for this:
• look hard at the first word;
• cover it over;
• visualise it;
• check that it has been visualised correctly;
• turn the page and write the word.

They should follow this method for all the words in their list. The children can then correct their own work.

Other spelling study sessions should follow the same pattern and children should try to concentrate on words they spelled incorrectly in the previous session.

The children should test their partners and mark the tests. Any words that are still misspelled should be carried forward and become the first word of next week's list.

9. Is spelling important?

Age range
Eight to twelve.

Group size
Groups of four.

What you need
Photocopiable page 184, felt-tipped pens, writing materials.

What to do
Ask the children each to write an answer to the question, 'Is spelling important?'. They should give two examples of situations when they think it is important, and two examples of occasions when it is not important. In their groups of four, the children can then pool their responses and discuss them.

The groups should then report back their discussion to the class. You can use the class discussion as an opportunity to point out that spelling matters more at some times than at others.

Finally, give each group a clean photocopiable page, and encourage the children to work collaboratively to write out their group's response. The filled-in photocopiable pages should then be mounted and displayed in the classroom.

10. Spelling, vocabulary and glossaries

Age range
Eight to twelve.

Group size
Individuals.

What you need
Books associated with children's hobbies, writing materials.

What to do
Interest in specialised vocabulary and the meaning of words associated with hobbies is a good way to focus children's attention on language. When studying and writing individual projects, they should be encouraged to make glossaries of vocabulary associated with the particular subject. These individually chosen words may then be used for spelling practice and for the study of regular and unusual patterns of words.

In a classroom that is alive with interest in new, unusual and long words and the patterns that occur within words, children respond warmly to such open tasks in language.

11. Making sense of nonsense

Age range
Nine to twelve.

Group size
Pairs.

What you need
Photocopiable page 185, writing materials.

What to do
Begin this activity by discussing full stops, commas, exclamation marks and capital letters with the children. Ask them what they mean, why they are used, and how and when to use them. The emphasis should be on *how* the writer uses these features to help the reader make sense of the text.

Introduce photocopiable page 185 and ask the children to work in pairs, each child reading the page to his or her partner. Ask the children to discuss the poem and try to make sense of the instructions given by the doctor. Allow just a few minutes for this.

Then discuss the poem as a whole class. Work out what the patient must do, according to the doctor, to become healthy. Ask the children to work in pairs and use the punctuation marks discussed earlier to try to make the phrasing of the instructions more obvious and, therefore, easier to understand.

Finally, ask the pairs to report back to the class. Different solutions should be encouraged and discussed. In particular, you should probe the reasoning behind the solutions proposed by the children, encouraging them to justify their decision.

12. Attitudes to spelling

Age range
Nine to twelve.

Group size
Groups of four or five.

What you need
Photocopiable page 186, writing materials, one A4 card per group, divided into halves labelled 'true' and 'false', sticky tape, scissors.

What to do
Give one copy of photocopiable page 186 to each child in the group and keep one additional copy to be used by the whole group in the second part of the activity.

Ask the children to consider the statements on the photocopiable page. They should individually decide whether each is true or false and record their decision by writing 'T' or 'F' beside each statement.

Ask the group as a whole to consider each statement in turn. The children should say what they have written on their individual decision sheets and why. The group must debate each statement and come to a group decision, cutting out each statement and using sticky tape to stick it on either the 'true' or the 'false' side of the paper.

This activity raises the issues surrounding the contentious subject of spelling and confronts attitudes head-on. It may also help dispel some of the children's misconceptions. Children should not, however, be left with the idea that it is impossible for people with spelling difficulties to improve their spelling, and it is suggested that Activities 9 and 10 on page 127 could be used to follow this activity.

13. Writing speeches: paragraphs

Age range
Nine to twelve.

Group size
Individuals.

What you need
Christmas tree lights, dressing-up clothes.

What to do
This activity will need several sessions. Writing speeches is an excellent way of encouraging children to examine their language very carefully, and consider the importance of using punctuation, grammar and paragraphs to give cues to the reader. Children hear speeches all the time, and can be taught several simple techniques to encourage good speech-writing. Once they become aware of these techniques, they are surprisingly quick to recognise them in speeches seen on television.

Although this activity is set within the context of switching on the Christmas tree lights, it can easily be adapted to suit any setting or context.

Begin by telling the children that there will be a tree-lighting ceremony in the town centre. Discuss the people who might be invited and the variety of local people who will be listening. Make a list of the dignitaries and celebrities who might make speeches; for example, the Lord Mayor, members of the Royal Family, local politicians, film stars, pop singers, representatives from schools or churches, and so on. Ask the children to decide which role they would like to play.

Next, discuss the symbolism of the occasion. Write a list on the chalkboard of all that the lights symbolise; for example, love, hope, security, light in the darkness, warmth, cheer, colour and so on.

Each child must then pick three main ideas and write a short paragraph about each. The paragraph should express their hopes for the future of their friends, their town and the world.

14. Writing speeches: punctuation

Age range
Nine to twelve.

Group size
Individuals.

What you need
Christmas tree lights, dressing-up clothes, writing materials.

What to do
Ask the children to imagine that they are to make a speech at the Christmas tree lighting ceremony. Let them look again at the paragraphs they wrote in Activity 13, and tell them that they are going to write these ideas into their speech. First, however, the class should discuss why people make speeches and what makes a good speech. It will be necessary to cover the following points.
• Speeches are made to communicate with an audience.
• Good speeches are short and entertaining.

• Good speeches appeal to people's emotions.
• Good speeches are written in a way that helps the reader read them effectively.

A speech begins with an address to the audience. All important dignitaries present should be named formally. On the chalkboard write a list of the names that might be mentioned. Ask individual children to read this list, telling the class to listen for the breaks and pauses which make the list both interesting to listen to and easy to understand. Explain how the use of punctuation can help the reader to read the list well.

It would be a good idea to read the children extracts from effective speeches, examining the techniques used by the speakers to appeal to the imagination and emotions of the crowd. Persuading words, such as 'Surely...', 'Clearly...' and 'Obviously...', are often used. Repetition of particular phrases is another common technique; for example, 'We shall fight them...' and 'I have a dream...'.

Rhetorical questions are also effective: 'Have you ever been cold? Have you ever been hungry? Have you ever had to go without your Christmas

dinner? Have you ever tried to survive with little money?'

Ask the children to write their speeches, and encourage them to practise reading them to a friend in the class. In order to make each technique effective, the speaker has to use the phrases correctly and pause for effect in the correct place. In reading, the children should note wherever they need to pause to emphasise a word or phrase, adding the appropriate punctuation to their written script.

Pick a few children to read the drafts of their speeches to the rest of the class. Discuss with them how to deliver the speeches effectively and how to indicate this in the script.

All the children should write the final versions of their speeches, and deliver them as the Christmas tree lights are switched on in the classroom. An invited audience of parents makes the ceremony more meaningful and, of course, it makes an excellent assembly!

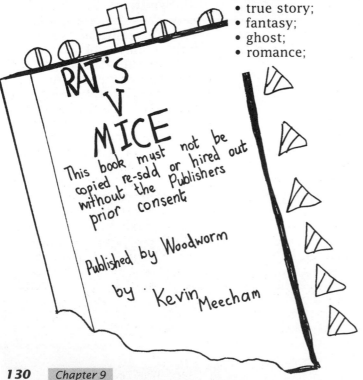

Conventions in context

1. Writing for infants

Age range
Six to twelve.

Group size
Individuals and pairs.

What you need
Writing materials.

What to do
Discuss with the children the many different types of story we read and list them on the chalkboard. The list will probably include some of the following:
• adventure;
• mystery;
• myth;
• legend;
• fable;
• true story;
• fantasy;
• ghost;
• romance;
• science fiction;
• autobiography;
• folk tale;
• fairy story.

Point out that the way the story is written depends on who the audience will be.

Tell the children that they are going to write a story for the younger infants in the school. Each child will draw the name of an infant out of a hat and this will be the person for whom they are going to write.

Ask each child to choose a writing partner in the class. Explain that writing partners should help each other by commenting helpfully on both the composing process and the conventions used in each other's stories.

From the list on the board, the children should decide which is the most appropriate type of story for infants.

The writing pairs should discuss:
• what sort of characters are appropriate and why;
• what length the story should be and why;
• how it should be illustrated;
• what sort of handwriting should be used;
• what sort of language should be used.

The children should be given time to write their story individually. You may like to allow a couple of thinking days before actually beginning the writing session. Tell them to think about the plot and the characters as they walk home, do the shopping, lie in bed at night, and so on.

Once the story has been written, it should be read aloud to the writing partner. The partner should then comment on, for example, the places where more expression, shorter sentences or pauses are required.

2. Story-boarding

Age range
Six to twelve.

Group size
Individuals and pairs.

What you need
Large sheets of paper folded into thirds, felt-tipped pens, writing materials.

What to do
Discuss the fact that all stories have a beginning, a middle and an end. The beginning introduces the characters and a 'problem' of some sort. The middle shows the characters trying to solve the problem, and the end indicates the final outcome.

Ask the children to divide the plots of their stories for the infants into a beginning, a middle and an end, illustrating the main point of each on the large sheets of paper.

Characters should be drawn with large speech bubbles coming out of their mouths, showing what they are saying at each point in the story. Remind the children that dragons, woodcutters, witches and princes speak in different ways. Discuss this and ask the children to give examples of the sort of differences there are in the ways people speak to each other.

The children should complete their story-boards, and finally show them to their writing partners.

3. Revising the conventions of direct speech

Age range
Six to twelve.

Group size
Individuals and pairs.

What you need
Scrap paper.

What to do
Remind the children that punctuation helps the reader to read a story. Because their stories are being written to be read aloud, it is very important that the reader knows how the writer wants it to be read.

The children will already have considered where the readers should pause in their stories, but they have not really considered how to indicate that the reader should 'put on a voice' for the listener.

Explain that it is impossible to put speech bubbles into a written story, but instead, the speech is 'held' in small marks called inverted commas. Take one child's story-board and show how speech marks are used to hold the spoken word.

Ask the children to write the words that are in speech bubbles on the story-board in speech marks on the back of the board. Because the reader no longer has the picture of the person to help him or her, they should indicate who is speaking and, for added effect, how the words were said. Emphasise that the author must tell the reader how to read the words in the story.

It is a good idea, at some point, to ask the children to make a list of all the different ways of delivering speech, and to display this in the classroom.

4. Redrafting the story

Age range
Six to twelve.

Group size
Individuals and pairs.

What you need
Writing materials, story drafts.

What to do
Having prepared and discussed their stories, the children should now return to their rough drafts and read them again. Talk to the children about how to alter or add to their stories, without having to copy the whole thing out again. Introduce conventions for altering a draft, for example:
• * for adding single words;
• // to indicate a new paragraph;
• arrows and circled pieces of writing to indicate changed word orders.

Put up a list of the drafting conventions to remind and help the class.

Older children can be shown how to cut and paste parts of the writing on to new sheets of paper so that new phrases and sentences can be written into the gaps. Tell them that parts may be discarded altogether.

If they have never been introduced to the idea that rewriting is not only acceptable but desirable, the children will be intrigued by the process.

Ask children to underline spellings that they have guessed, or that they think do not look quite right. This will remind them to check these words at a later date. They should also decide how they are going to divide the story into pages, planning the number of pages and where the divisions will come.

5. Presenting the book

Age range
Six to twelve.

Group size
Individuals and pairs.

What you need
Very best quality drawing and writing materials.

What to do
Some children who are not familiar with the redrafting process may be worried about the rough state of their writing.

When the audience is real, and the composing process has taken some effort, surface features of presentation take on additional importance. The writing, pictures and general presentation have to be perfect in order to reflect the unseen effort of the composing process.

In their writing pairs, the children will have to make the following decisions:
• What size will the book be?
• How many illustrations will it have?
• Where will they appear?
• Will illuminated lettering be used?
• How large will the writing be?
• How will the writing be kept straight?

It is a good idea to photocopy 'underlays' of thick black lines to go under plain paper. Give children a choice of different widths and ensure that these are always available in the classroom, along with paper-clips to keep the writing paper and underlay together.

All decisions about presentation must be made before the redrafting is started. Children usually enjoy this activity, since it is purposeful and the industry of careful writing is relieved at regular intervals with illustrations.

Finally, a beautifully decorated dedication and title page should be made for the book, and of course a cover. Authors may like to write a piece about themselves and find a small photograph for the back cover.

When all books are completed, an event should be organised in which the authors read their books to the younger children for whom they were written. Perhaps a photocopy of each book could be made to give to the infant.

CHAPTER 10

Publication and display

In order for children to write well, they need a clear sense of their audience. Watching others react to their work provides information about what works with readers and what doesn't. This is the essential feedback which all writers need in order to develop and refine their craft.

The publication and display of written work should not be considered the 'cherry on the cake' which is enjoyed most frequently by an élite of 'good writers' in the class. It is an educational tool, important for all children, but perhaps most important for those with the poorest sense of audience and purpose in their writing.

Devoting space and time to displaying children's work raises the status of such work in the classroom. It is a celebration of effort and achievement which no teacher can afford to ignore.

However, there is another absolutely fundamental reason for encouraging children to read each other's work. Through reading their own and each other's work, the children develop a more sophisticated understanding of what reading and writing are all about. They become more aware of the decisions made by the writer in all that they read. This happens because when a child rereads a story that she has written or watched a friend write, she reads with the author's questions fresh in her mind. This memory of the process of composing encourages the child to appreciate not only the story, but also the skill with which the writer went about telling it.

BACKGROUND

Publication and display

Displays in the classroom have usually been chosen, designed and erected by the teacher, and generally serve an identifiable purpose. For example, the purpose might be to:
• show the work of the class to the rest of the school;
• encourage interest in a topic;
• encourage or reward the efforts of individuals;
• set a standard of work for the class;
• brighten a dull or under-used corner.

Displays must be changed regularly, or they cease to be noticed.

Publication, however, should be seen as the final outcome of the writing process, and is primarily the child's responsibility. Publication is important because it gives the child control over what happens to a particular piece of work. The child decides which pieces of work should be published, the format to be used and the style and number of illustrations.

Unlike display, publication is permanent, providing a lasting record of achievement. It can be a reference point for later work, and can point up development. It allows the children to review and revisit old pieces written by themselves and others.

Publication should be a regular, although not an automatic, part of the writing process. Younger children will be likely to publish more pieces of work than older ones, who tend to spend longer refining and rewriting a single piece.

What should be displayed or published?

The short answer is – anything at all! The important thing is that, if the display is to be noticed and read by the children, it must be discussed and included in classwork wherever possible.

Apart from the usual displays on topics covered in class, displays can illustrate the writing process by showing several drafts of a single piece of work, or can be used as a basis for further work.

Towards the end of the school year, displays can show progression and development by showing a selection of work from the beginning, middle and end of the year.

Problems with display and publishing

Putting up displays undoubtedly takes up a lot of teacher time. Once children understand the purpose, design and colour-scheme of an intended display, they can be taught to mount their own work, which leaves the teacher with the comparatively quick job of putting it up. Obviously, this requires a place in the classroom where work can be mounted, as well as a regular place to store finished items. 'Instant' display techniques, such as using brightly coloured binding tape to edge younger children's work, can produce acceptable results very quickly.

The limitations

While it is true that display and publishing help develop a variety of positive attitudes towards writing, it must be remembered that children take their cues from the whole picture, not just 'snapshots'. Thus, no amount of time or fuss over displays will make up for a lack of time spent in discussion and appreciation of the children's efforts during the writing process.

ACTIVITIES

1. Raising awareness

Age range
Five to twelve.

Group size
Individuals, pairs or the whole class.

What you need
Writing materials.

What to do
Talk to the class about the displays they can see in their own classroom. Not all young children make the connection between the work they or their friends have done and that which they see beautifully mounted and displayed on the classroom walls, so ask if they can recall when and how particular pieces of work were done. To assess their general awareness, ask them which display has been up the longest and what was there before the current display.

Discuss the displays on the wall. Ask which the children like most, and why. If they have a piece of work on the wall at that time, how did they feel when they first saw it up, and has anyone else commented on it? How did this make them feel? Have they ever commented on other people's work on the wall, and if so, when, and what did they say (and if not, why not)?

Now ask the children what other displays they can remember seeing around the school, and ask them to describe these to the rest of the class. Do they know which classes did the work for particular displays? How would they guess? Try to probe the children to find out exactly what they have noticed and understood.

Take the class on a walk around the school, looking particularly at the displays. Stop frequently to allow the children to observe, ask questions and comment on what they see. Use the opportunity to raise issues which can be followed up later. Who do the children think the displays are for? Do they all serve the same purpose? What makes a good display? Why? How can they tell what age-group produced the work for a particular display? Finally, ask the children to say which display they found most interesting and why.

On returning to the classroom, the children can write or draw about a display that they particularly remember and say why. They could also write cards or letters of appreciation to the class involved.

Further activity
A discussion of what makes a particular classroom look welcoming could lead to the children suggesting practical ways to improve their own classroom environment.

2. Mounting work

Age range
Six to twelve.

Group size
Individuals and pairs.

What you need
Work to mount, mounting paper, child-safe cutters, a selection of good and bad examples of mounting, colour choice, double-mounting and 'edging'.

What to do
Begin by putting all the examples you have collected on the wall, where they can be clearly seen by the children.

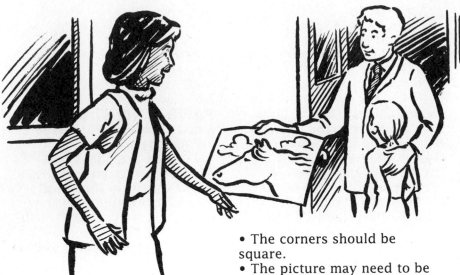

Label each example and ask the children to work in pairs and consider each picture in turn. They are to decide whether they think the picture is mounted well or badly. Older children must justify their decision by listing the good and bad points about each.

Use the first picture for a class discussion. Make it clear that children are not to comment on the quality of the picture itself, but on how it is mounted and displayed.

Allow the class a reasonable amount of time to do this, depending on how many examples you have displayed. Then discuss each picture in turn, asking the children to report their opinions to the class. From this discussion, draw out the main teaching points about how to mount a picture well and list these on the board. You will probably mention some or all of the following features.

• The edge of both picture and mount should be trimmed to leave a clean, neat edge.

• The corners should be square.
• The picture may need to be cut down to size.
• The mounting paper should complement the colours in the picture.
• The picture must be placed on the mount with equal margins on either side. It may have less margin above than below, or an equal margin above and below.
• Double mounting, with a narrow black or brightly coloured border around the picture contrasting with the broader mount, can look effective.
• It is important to use an appropriate adhesive, which does not wrinkle the picture as it dries.

Ask the children to choose (or select for each child) a piece of work to mount. They are to choose the mounting paper and do all the measuring and cutting to size. Emphasise the importance of using paper economically, and of clearing up after themselves. Explain what to do with left-over scraps of different sizes. (It is a good idea to have a drawer for 'useful scraps' and a collage drawer – or the rubbish bin – for those bits that are too small to be of any use.)

Afterwards, ask the children to comment on and assess their work.

3. Work from home

Age range
Five to twelve.

Group size
Individuals or the whole class.

What you need
A defined and labelled area of the classroom wall.

What to do
By allowing a space in school for the display of work done at home, a teacher is implicitly sending messages to the class about the value placed on children's experiences outside school. It reinforces the links between home and school, and helps meet the need of many children to find a wider audience for work of which they are proud, but which they happen not to have done at school.

The bulletin board can be managed in several different ways. Initially, you could just make the space available to the children and discuss with them the sort of work they might like to bring in.

Make sure that you continue to take an interest in specific pieces of work and comment on them. Encourage the children to maintain a high standard of mounting and display.

If the space is either very popular or the idea does not really take off, you might like to suggest that a group of children become the bulletin board 'editors'. Their responsibility will be to seek samples of work from class members, to ensure a wide variety of work and to make sure that displays are regularly changed. Each group should only be responsible for a limited period and must be given specific instructions about their duties and responsibilities.

4. A place to hide

Age range
Five to twelve.

Group size
Small groups and the whole class.

What you need
Two long tables, a roll of fabric or crêpe paper, newspaper, sticky tape, staples.

What to do
Children love the idea of 'dens', and it is good to harness this enthusiasm in the interests of education!

Place one of the tables against a wall, preferably with an electric point nearby so that a lamp may be pulled through into the den. Place the second table in front of the first so that they meet.

Make a deep cavern between the back wall and the front table by draping the material or crêpe paper over the top and sides of the tables, securing it with drawing pins, staples or sticky tape. Overlapping layers of scrunched-up newspapers beneath the material should give the effect of a rocky cave. The material should be secure under the top edge of the front table and around its legs to form the entrance of a cave.

Similar effects can be gained using chicken wire covered with papier mâché or large sheets of thick plastic sprayed with silver and gold paint.

It is worthwhile taking time and trouble over this display because over the course of a year it can be used in many different ways – it is

surprisingly easy to build a 'den' idea into any project. It could be:
• a coal or gold mine;
• an animal home;
• another land;
• the home of a magical creature;
• a secret hideout;
• Santa's grotto.

The possibilities are endless. Appropriate art and craft work or writing can be displayed on the surfaces and the walls or hung from the roof of the den. If carpet is placed on the floor inside, children can use it as a retreat in which to work or read quietly.

5. Interactive displays

Age range
Five to twelve.

Group size
Six groups of four to six children.

What you need
Art and writing materials, a den (see Activity 4) or corner of the classroom.

What to do
Explain to the children that the den you have built in the classroom (lit from within by a lamp or large torch, for effect) is really a magic cave in a magic land inhabited by

The Stone-Age

strange creatures. Other beings live on the land above the cave, but neither populace knows about the other.

The children are going to invent the inhabitants of this magic land. Each group will have responsibility for one area of the display; the air, the ground, the roof of the cave, the sides, and the land above the cave. Each child must make a creature or plant which lives in their area. They may use collage, model-making or art techniques. As they make their creature, they must think of the following points:
• What does it need to survive?
• How does it get its food?
• How does it see, hear and defend itself?
• How and where does it sleep?
• Does it always remain in the cave, and if so, why?
• What magic powers does it possess?

Once the creatures have been made, the children should describe them, using the points above to help them. The creatures should be mounted in the correct place on the display. Roof-creatures should be hung as mobiles from the underside of the table and figures living on the floor or top of the cave can be mounted on to the sides of boxes and stood in place. The descriptive writing can be added to the display.

To familiarise everyone with the two lands and their inhabitants, each group should select investigators to explore particular areas, make notes on what they see and read and report back to the rest of the group.

Further activity
This can be the beginning of an imaginative adventure story, as described in Chapter 5.

6. Writing cubes

Age range
Five to twelve.

Group size
Groups of five or six.

What you need
Cardboard boxes, wrapping paper, pieces of writing.

What to do
Show the children how to select a suitable box of the right size and shape. This will, of course, depend on the work to be displayed. Ensure that all the sides are firmly secured with sticky tape before covering the box with the wrapping paper, as if wrapping a parcel.

Then ask the children to consider which colour mounting paper would best contrast or tone with the wrapping paper, and let them mount their work. Remind them that toning colours generally look most effective when teamed with black as a double mount.

One piece of work may be mounted on each face of the box. This technique can be used by a group to display several pieces of writing on a theme, or by an individual or pairs of children to display the separate chapters of a story. Boxes may be stacked on top of each other or hung from the ceiling on lengths of string.

Other interesting shapes can also be used, and this can link with maths work. The children could, for example, make and use triangular or square-based pyramids, displaying a piece of writing on each face.

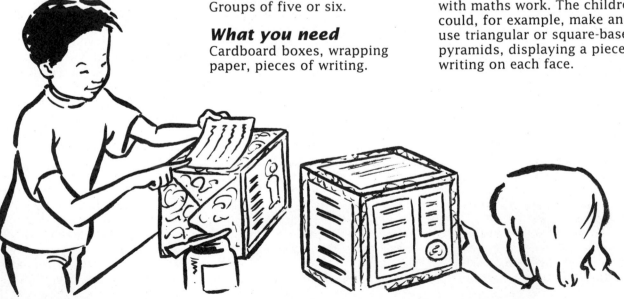

7. Advent calendar

Age range
Seven to twelve.

Group size
Individuals and the whole class.

What you need
Two pieces of A1 card, smaller pieces of card, 6cm squares of paper, 8cm squares of card, gold and silver pens, carpet knife, writing and art materials, Blu-Tack, sticky tape, current newspapers.

What to do
Towards the end of November, tell the class that they are going to make an advent calendar. On one of the A1 sheets of card, draw a large picture of a Christmassy subject such as Santa, the crib, an angel or a Christmas tree. This is your contribution to the art work.

Over the course of the next week, in their spare time, the children should each draw and make their own object to add to the picture, thus building up a huge composite class picture. Other members of staff or visitors may also be invited to contribute.

Ask the children each to make a small picture on an 8cm square of card, illustrating one aspect of Christmas. Now discuss the meaning of Christmas with the class. Ask each child to write a Christmas wish for the class, the school, the town or the world in the coming year. Give them the 6cm squares of paper on which to do this. Older children may get ideas by looking through newspapers.

Once they have written their wishes, the children should fold them in half and stick them with Blu-Tack on to their pictures.

The pictures and wishes should then be stuck face down with sticky tape on to the back of the composite Christmas picture.

Using a carpet knife, score around the outline of the pictures, cutting into the card of the large picture so that each small picture has a 'door' in front of it. Staple the whole picture on to the blank A1 card, to make a basic (but very large) advent calendar.

From 1 December onwards, one or two doors can be opened each day. A short wish-reading ceremony adds to the occasion. The children will not know where in the advent calendar their pictures and writing are situated, and will become very excited wondering whose Christmas work is to be revealed when a door is opened.

8. Analysis of a display

Age range
Eight to twelve.

Group size
Individuals and pairs.

What you need
Access to displays, writing materials.

What to do
Talk to the class about the displays they can see in their own classroom, and those they can recall seing around the school.

Ask the class how important they think it is to display work well. Of the displays they have seen recently, which do they feel are particularly effective and eye-catching?

Try to get them to analyse and explain why this is so. It may be because of the colours, the contrasts, the interesting materials or shapes, or it may be because of the nature of the work itself.

Suggest to the class that it is particularly difficult to get passers-by to read written work on the walls, but that some forms of display are more successful than others. Put the class into pairs and take them on a tour of the school. Either tell each pair to find one display that they think is particularly effective, or assign each pair to a particular display. Tell them to spend some time looking at it, and ask them to comment on the following aspects.
• How are colour, texture and shape used?
• How do these things make an impact, catch the eye or unify the display?
• How are individual pieces of work mounted? (See the teaching points for Activity 2 on page 135.)
• How good is the overall organisation and layout of the work? Are items arranged with care, in an attractive, orderly way? Are they well-spaced with a clear border around the edge of the display board?
• Are the labels and notices informative, unambiguous, neat and easy to read?
• What types of work are on display?

If possible, let the children take a photograph or make a sketch of the whole display. Underneath this, they should brainstorm all their first impressions and comments on the display. Children should be encouraged to find out who put up the display, and to interview the children and teacher to find out what they think about it.

This work should be written up by older children in the form of a report. Younger ones could perhaps write a letter to the teacher and class responsible for the display, telling them what they liked about it and why.

Finally, the whole class should take part in a guided tour of display in the school, each pair taking it in turns to talk about the display they have been investigating.

9. Less is sometimes more!

Age range
Eight to twelve.

Group size
Individuals.

What you need
Thick card, coloured paper, poems, tissues, fabric, adhesive, scissors, gold lettering pens.

What to do
Children are fascinated by miniature books. This activity offers a good opportunity to show how display can be used to focus attention on a few specially selected items which might be missed in a more crowded setting. It is particularly effective for drawing attention to poems or lines of poetry.

About a week before the lesson, ask the children to find a special poem or line of poetry. It can be a poem they have written, a poem they particularly like, or the favourite poem of a friend or relative. The important thing is that they should have read and thought about a particular poem or line of poetry.

Each child in the class could make a small book about 10cm square, as described in Activity 14 on page 143. The layout of the first page, showing the title, dedication and publisher's logo, should be planned in rough before being copied neatly on to the first page of the book.

The next two or three pages should contain the chosen poem, or some lines from it, copied out neatly, with a decorated border and illustrations if space allows. Again, children will need to plan the layout of each page and decide where to make any necessary breaks in the poem before copying it out.

10. Authors of the week

Age range
Nine to twelve (or younger children with teacher's help – see further activity).

Group size
Pairs or threes.

What you need
Wall space, photographs of children, children's work, labels for sections: 'finished work', 'work in progress', 'ideas for future work'.

What to do
Once the children have been writing for some time they will have amassed a backlog of work and will be beginning to take an 'insider's view' of writing and authorship, developing an interest in both the writing process and the work of their classmates. Suggest that they now need more opportunity to read each other's work and share ideas for future work.

Explain that the classroom wall display will feature a section on 'Authors of the week'. Each week, two or three children will have an opportunity to display work in varying stages of completion. Children will know in advance when their week will be, and with whom they will share it, because each will be asked to 'sign up' for the particular week they would like to do.

Each author will take responsibility for her own display. She must decide which pieces of work will be displayed and how they will be mounted and arranged on the wall. Each display will also have a photograph of the children involved and a short piece entitled 'About the authors'.

This is a good opportunity for the children to put into practice many of the aspects of good display that they have been considering. As the teacher, you may like to place a constraint on either the amount of display space or the number of pieces per author.

Further activity
This idea can also be used with younger children, with teacher help to decide what work should be displayed and how. They could also collaborate in writing the information about the authors.

11. Display ideas bank

Age range
Nine to twelve.

Group size
Groups of four.

What you need
Card, thick felt-tipped pens, rulers, scissors, 'pop-up' books such as *How Many Bugs in a Box?* by David A. Carter (Orchard Books), or *Fungus the Bogeyman Plop-up Book* by Raymond Briggs (Hamish Hamilton).

What to do
Talk to the children about enticing others to read work on display. Ask what the problems are – it may be because of the location or position of display boards, or because the displays themselves are not enticing enough.

Ask the children to think of different ways to display their work. They could use a variety of flaps, three-dimensional displays or roller displays to try to make the reader as active as possible. Some of the techniques used in the pop-up books might be useful sources of inspiration.

Each group should be given one sheet of A1 card, plus as many other smaller pieces as are needed. Each child must look through his or her writing, choose the best piece of work and decide how to display it. Every member of the group must display their work on the A1 card in a different way. (The illustration gives a variety of ideas.)

You will have to explain how to write or trace notices and headings on to separate pieces of paper before mounting these and sticking them in the appropriate place.

12. The 'good display' book

Age range
Nine to twelve.

Group size
Pairs and the whole class.

What you need
Camera and film, large blank book, paper.

What to do
This is a book which can be started with the whole class, and then added to periodically by individual children. Begin by raising the children's awareness of aspects of effective display. This could be done with a class tour of the school, or one of the other activities mentioned in this chapter. Encourage the children to list and analyse the important aspects. The list might include:
• location;
• use of colour;
• use of shape;
• layout and organisation;
• use of labelling;
• use of three-dimensional effects;
• selection and quality of work.

Each item on the list should have a section of the book devoted to it. Pairs of children should be allocated to a particular section, and asked to look around and find one display which is a good example to illustrate their section. This may take several days or weeks. Once they have identified the display, they must photograph it and write a few sentences saying why their chosen aspect is so impressive.

13. Zigzag books

Age range
Five to twelve.

Group size
Individuals.

What you need
Strips of card 10 to 20cm wide, paper, rulers, scissors.

What to do
Let the children decide how many pages will be needed and divide the strip of card accordingly. They should fold along each divide, bending the folds in alternate directions to produce a concertina-like effect. Very thick card may need to be scored with the scissors and ruler before being bent. (Note that the score-line should be on the outside of each fold, and will therefore have to be done on alternate sides of the strip.)

Writing may be displayed on each face of the book and then folded away. The title should be beautifully decorated, and should of course be on the uppermost 'page' of the book.

Zigzag books may be used to display work by one child or a whole class. The pages may be written or drawn on, or work can be stuck in. The books can be displayed flat, or one end can be stapled firmly to the wall so that readers can extend the pages.

14. Bound books

Age range
Five to twelve.

Group size
Individuals.

What you need
Cardboard, wide binding tape, wallpaper, fabric, paint, wrapping paper, lettering stencils, needles, thread.

What to do
Making and binding books takes time, and it is a good idea to make a supply of books before the start of each term. Alternatively, you could set aside an afternoon and show the children how to make several books of their own.

To make a book, first decide how large it is going to be, and cut two pieces of thick cardboard to the right size and shape. Choose a covering – wallpaper, wrapping paper, fabric, or paper previously painted or stencilled.

To make the front and back covers, lay the pieces of cardboard flat with a space of about 5mm between them. Tape the pieces together using the wide binding tape, making sure to preserve the small gap between the pieces of card. For added strength, tape both sides of the card.

Place the card on to the material with which it is to be covered. There should be about 2.5cm of material spare all the way around. Fold down the corners of the covering material and stick or tape these on to the card. Then, as if wrapping a parcel, fold down each edge, sticking and taping it firmly into place.

Finally, to produce a good finish on the inside cover of each book, stick two pieces of toning paper on to the exposed cardboard, hiding the taped edges of the covering material.

To make the inside pages, choose plain or lined paper that, when folded in half, is slightly smaller than the outside cover. Sew or staple these into the book.

Further activity
Smaller books look and feel very special if, before they are covered in fabric, the outer faces are padded with tissues.

15. Personalised jotters

Age range
Five to twelve.

Group size
Individuals.

What you need
Commercially produced jotters, card cut to size of jotter, adhesive, writing and colouring materials.

What to do
A good way to encourage a high standard of presentation in any project jotter is to tell the children before they begin their work that the jotter is to be presented as a gift to someone they like a great deal.

Show the children the dedication page from a novel such as *The Lion, The Witch and The Wardrobe*, by C. S. Lewis – this one is particularly interesting. Stress what an honour it is to have a book dedicated to you.

Ask the children to leave the first three pages of the jotter blank, beginning their work on the fourth page. The initial pages will be used to write the title page, contents list and, of course, the dedication. Explain that the children will be making beautiful covers for the books once they have finished writing them. Keep reminding them as they work that this book is for someone special, giving plenty of positive rather than negative criticism, thus encouraging their best efforts.

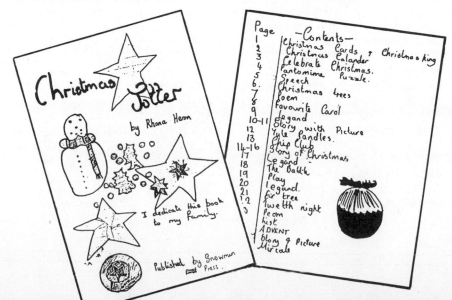

At the end of the project, the children should be asked to number the pages of their books and complete the first three pages.

Ask the children to design a front and back cover for their books, and give them pieces of card on which to do this. Finally, stick the card over the front and back covers of the jotter. Complete the effect by threading a string of finger-knitting or knotted thread through the centre pages and tying it, so that the jotters may be hung on display before being taken home and presented to the people to whom they were dedicated.

16. Publishing work

Age range
Seven to twelve.

Group size
Individuals and pairs.

What you need
Photocopiable page 189 (if required), class written work.

What to do
Although children should often be given the opportunity to read, discuss and display their writing, not every piece of work that a child does will be published in permanent form as a book. Publishing is a special event and should only be done with pieces of work which the child considers very special and worthy of being recorded for ever. Older children may only publish once or twice a year.

It is often a good idea to introduce the idea of publishing, explain the process to the whole class and give each child an opportunity to experience it first of all.

Begin by asking the children to consider all the individual pieces of work they have done in the past. Ask them to select two pieces which they think are good and might be of interest to other readers; in other words, two pieces they would consider publishing.

Ask the children to share these pieces of work with a partner. They should read their work out loud first, and say why each piece was chosen. The pair must discuss which of the pieces is most suitable for publication, although the final decision must rest with the writer. Emphasise the importance of being constructive when commenting on someone else's work.

You may like to use photocopiable page 189 as a means of structuring these discussions. The most effective way of showing the children how to use the sheet may be for you to play the part of a 'partner' and demonstrate its use in front of the whole class.

As with the original selection of material, partners must realise that they may suggest alterations, but the writer has the final say over what happens to the work.

Once the work has been edited by the children, it should be attached to the completed photocopiable sheet and placed in a box labelled 'Work to be published', for you to read and check.

Children may then begin to make and cover their books.

Further activity
Eventually the children can be taught to edit their work without the aid of a partner. They can be shown how to skim a piece, as a reader might, to see if the language is clear and the ideas coherent. They could consider the opening sentences critically, possibly rewriting them in a more exciting way, or use a pencil to check for spelling errors word by word. Remember, however, that it is not realistic to expect children to suddenly take on board and use all these techniques at once; the different strategies should be introduced one at a time.

17. Publishing formats

Age range
Seven to twelve.

Group size
Individuals and the whole class.

What you need
Home-made and professionally published books (various sizes, typefaces and layouts), blank samples of home-made books (different sizes and bindings), rough paper for notes if required.

What to do
Show the collection of published books to the class. Point out the different sizes, typefaces and page lengths, and the number of illustrations. Explain that after (or sometimes before) each book was written, the authors and publishers had to choose how the book would look when it was published. Select a couple of books to use as examples, and ask the class to suggest why the format is especially suitable for that type of story or book.

When you feel that the children understand what is required, ask them to work in pairs and look at the books provided, deciding why the author and publisher chose particular formats. Tell the children that they will not have time to look at all the books, but they should consider as many formats as possible. You may like to issue older children with rough paper and suggest that they jot down any points they would like to make.

After about 20 minutes, ask the children to comment on what they have seen. Introduce the blank samples and remind the class how each was made. Suggest that when they next want to publish their work, they consider which format would be most appropriate.

Further activity
Give each group of two or three children a script written by you or a child. You may tell them which age group it has been written for, or ask them to decide this themselves. Tell them that they are to publish this in the most suitable way possible. They must read it carefully, decide how they will divide it into pages and then choose the most suitable format in which to publish it.

This task will take several sessions. Once all groups have finished, they should be asked to read and comment on the work produced by other groups in the class.

18. Publish or display?

Age range
Eight to twelve.

Group size
Individuals and pairs.

What you need
Spare paper, display-sized paper, marker pen.

What to do
It is very important that all children are given the opportunity to display or publish their work. Indeed, it could be argued that publishing or displaying work is most important for those children who have the least confidence in their abilities.

Children need to understand the difference between publication and display, and must be able to choose the most appropriate method for broadcasting the good work they do.

Begin by discussing the differences between books and work displayed on the wall. Obviously the type and range of audience they will reach, the speed with which they can be produced and, in some cases, the type of work will be different. Try to make the point that the more permanent the display method, the better the work must be.

Get half the class to list all the processes which might precede the publication of a book and the other half to list the processes which precede the display of a piece of work. Collate the lists and display these in the classroom. Suggest that the children use the lists to decide whether a piece of work is more suitable for publishing or for displaying.

Further activity
Children can be asked to find one piece of work they would like to publish and one piece they would like to display. They should present and explain their choices to the rest of the group.

CHAPTER 11

Recording and assessment

Assessment is currently one of the most controversial aspects of teaching. The debate is highly charged because the issue has been strongly linked to that of standards of learning and teaching in schools. Other issues, such as the role of parents and the government have further complicated the arguments about what should be assessed, when and how assessment should be made, and for what purposes.

Clearly, it is outside the scope of this book to enter into the debate. However, it is important to think clearly about the type of information that teachers and children need on a regular, day-to-day basis to advance learning. It is this that we hope to clarify.

BACKGROUND

Why is assessment important?

Effective assessment is essential if teaching is to be effective.

Through skilled observation and questioning, the teacher should be able to decide what a child can do well and what he or she has yet to learn. It is here that assessment can make the most difference, since it helps teachers to decide what a child needs to do today, tomorrow, this week or this month in order to take his or her writing forward.

Assessment also teaches children to recognise and celebrate good work. Through sharing quality work with the class, teachers are able to set high standards and encourage others to aspire to them. Discussion at a class or group level encourages the children to develop a critical appreciation which informs their own writing, while assessment of an individual piece of writing provides feedback and indicates ways forward for the child, raising his or her confidence and motivation.

What makes assessment effective?

Effective assessment always has a purpose which is clearly understood by both the teacher and the child. The child understands the criteria on which the assessment is based, and is able to link this to its purpose, resulting in action designed to take the child's writing forward.

Children and teachers should regard assessment as positively helpful. Thus, any programme of work or action arising from assessment should be devised in consultation with the child and be seen by him or her as achievable. The most productive assessments are tightly focused, pointing to just one or two features of the writing which require attention. Any more than this tends to have a negative effect, overwhelming the writer.

If children really understand the purpose and reasoning behind the assessment, they will often be able to suggest ways forward, and this should be encouraged. No child should be left after an assessment not knowing what is good about his or her writing, or unable to envisage how it might be improved. It is the teacher's job, through discussion, to help the child find new ways forward.

Speech bubble: *How do you feel about ...?*

How should writing be assessed?

Obviously, teachers need to assess and record how children are progressing in their writing. Different features of writing will be assessed and recorded in different ways; thus spelling or the use of other conventions will be assessed differently from the quality of expression, the individuality or the range of strategies used by a child.

Some features can be assessed by tests, some by keeping checklists and still others through holding writing conferences and discussing the work with the child.

Assess the whole child

Consider the child's concept of self and concept of writing. Does she see herself as a natural writer, occasionally experiencing problems which will be surmounted, or does she see little purpose in writing, have little sense of audience, and see it as a magical gift which others have but she lacks? How aware is the child of her control over language and the writing process? What critical awareness does she have? What range of topics does she feel happy with as a writer, and what particular interests inform her writing?

Keep conventions and composing separate

Surface features of writing, such as grammar, spelling, handwriting, length and general neatness, are all fairly easy to discuss and 'mark' because they are there on the page for both you and the child to see. More abstract features such as whether the child writes with a distinctive and personal voice, how he orders and develops ideas or the skill with which he selects and uses language are equally, if not more, important and must also be considered.

Assess the process as well as the product

Writing should be considered in the context in which it was done. Teachers are often good talkers, but not such good listeners. Yet how can you judge the success of a piece of writing if you know nothing of the intentions of the writer, or of the difficulties encountered? Only by asking the child will you understand how she perceives the finished product and how well it matches her original intentions. Only by discussing the writing process will you understand *why* the child feels as she does about the work.

Variable quality can be healthy!

Writing rarely improves in a steady, linear fashion, with each new work surpassing the last. Progress is erratic, with rapid development often being followed by a consolidation period, and sometimes the quality of the work may even appear to diminish as the writer seeks to apply and test new ideas and techniques across a range of topics.

Teachers must accept this, and expect the quality of written work to vary. Indeed, this can be a sign of good teaching, showing that the child has both the confidence and the independence to explore the applications of what has been learned. Clearly,

children who are given a breadth of writing experience and are encouraged to stretch themselves will meet with both successes and failures. The highest quality work comes from children who are prepared to take risks; inquiring, independent learners, intent on discovering the possibilities within the work rather than playing safe by writing what they think the teacher wants to read.

Other, external factors also affect the quality of writing, some of which are outside the teacher's control – the topic, the child's mood and competing distractions in the child's psyche can all play their part in determining the quality of work produced.

It is important that teachers recognise and monitor healthy variability in children's work and consider the reasons underlying it. Likewise, they should be aware of those children who seem to be on a 'downward spiral', those who rarely produce quality work, or those who limit their writing to a narrow range of familar topics or styles.

Keeping records

Teachers need records of children's achievements in writing. Apart from ongoing class records, and the records that children keep about their work, it is a worthwhile exercise to make a point of considering the progress individual children have made each term or half-term. There are nearly always some surprises – children who have made little progress yet escaped your attention, or children who have improved in leaps and bounds and you'd forgotten by just how much. Of course, the results of these retrospective assessments give much pleasure when shared with the writers themselves.

The need for a whole-school policy

In order for children to do well, it is necessary for them to have some continuity as they move up the school. Of course, not all teachers are going to teach the same way, and it would not be to the children's benefit if they did. However, teachers should agree on the basic principles of what should be taught and assessed.

Devising a whole-school writing policy is one way in which teachers can discuss what they do and what they believe to be important about teaching writing. From this the school can decide what teachers need to know about individuals as writers, and can agree the form and format of school records.

There is no one right way to keep records, and the data will reflect the individual school's policy. Some schools keep samples of work, some keep written records under headings for voice, skill, confidence and conventions, and still others use tick-charts, or a mixture of recording methods.

The one golden rule is that records are only useful if they are read. Excessively complex or lengthy records do not benefit child or teacher.

Not only teachers assess

As soon as children become aware that others have opinions and judge their work, they become vulnerable to those judgements. Parents, peers, siblings and a whole host of others all judge work and judge it differently. Whatever criteria they use, their opinions are often very influential when heard through the ears of a child. When the criteria used by the home or peer group are very different from those of the school or the teacher, the conflict can put undue pressure on a child, sapping confidence and enjoyment.

ACTIVITIES

1. Teacher/child work record

Age range
Seven to twelve.

Group size
Individuals and pairs.

What you need
Photocopiable page 187, writing materials, paper.

What to do
Begin the lesson by telling the children that you are going to ask them to think about the writing they have done recently. Give the children a sheet of paper each and tell them to write on it their name and the title of a piece of writing which they found really difficult. In pairs, ask the children to share their titles and discuss why the pieces were so difficult. Then ask individuals to share with the class their thoughts about why some writing is more difficult than others. Write these ideas on the chalkboard.

Now tell the class to think of a piece of writing with which they were really pleased and to write down its title. Ask them to tell their partner why they were pleased with it. Again, ask individuals to report to the class, and record their comments on the chalkboard.

Ask the children whether they think it is possible to find a piece of writing very hard, but finally do it well and be really pleased with the result.

Listen to the responses, and encourage the children to give reasons and examples of work they have done in the past to illustrate their point. Similarly, if a piece of work is very easy, are the children more or less likely to be really satisfied with it? Again, probe their answers.

Introduce photocopiable page 187 and explain that you want to know what the children think of the work they have done in the past few months. You want to know how difficult they found it and also how satisfied they were with the end result. Ask the children to review their workbooks and list the titles. Then ask them to grade each piece on a scale of zero to five; zero for 'easy' or 'not pleased', and five for 'hard' or 'very pleased'.

While the children are doing this, take the opportunity to discuss with individuals the relationship between the amount of struggle and the amount of satisfaction. End the lesson by posing this question generally to the class, asking children to find examples from the titles in front of them to justify their opinions.

2. Assessment criteria

Age range
Seven to twelve.

Group size
The whole class.

What you need
Chalkboard, large sheets of paper, marker pens.

What to do
With the class, brainstorm all the different criteria that the children think teachers might use to judge their work. Working from this list, ask individuals to choose the four criteria which they think teachers would rate as most important, and to list these in order of priority. Ask individuals to share their lists with the class, saying why they placed them in that order.

3. Best work album

Age range
Six to twelve.

Group size
Individuals.

What you need
Large scrapbook, albums or hardcover books.

What to do
Either give out, or get each child to make, a large hardcover book with about five or six pages in it. Explain that once a month the children will be asked to choose the best piece of work they have done that month. They will mount it (using a photocopy, if this is more convenient) and put it into their album. At the end of the year, they should have about ten pieces of work which celebrate their achievements over the year.

4. Attention to detail

Age range
Five to twelve.

Group size
Individuals.

What you need
Handwriting book, handwriting exercises.

What to do
At the end of each handwriting lesson, ask the children to decide which line or letter is their overall best, and to indicate this with a small star. When looking through the books with the children, ask them why they chose that particular line above the others. Use this as an opportunity to comment positively on children's strengths, and to identify areas for future improvement.

If done regularly, this provides a very good baseline against which children can measure the improvement in their handwriting. Children should be encouraged to look at each other's handwriting and to discuss the lines and letters they chose as the best.

5. Celebration of achievements

Age range
Six to twelve.

Group size
Individuals.

What you need
Photocopiable page 188.

What to do
Stick copies of photocopiable page 188 on to the inside cover of each child's writing book. Explain to them that you are going to list all the conventions that you notice the child using correctly. In order for a convention to be listed on the certificate, children must consistently use it correctly in their own writing, without being reminded. As children start to identify and regularly use new conventions, these should be added to the list on the sheet.

6. Mark your own

Age range
Eight to twelve.

Group size
Individuals.

What you need
Photocopiable page 189, children's work.

What to do
You may need to add to or delete some of the criteria on page 189 to suit the needs of the class. Introduce the photocopiable sheets and explain what is meant by each of the headings. Tell the

children that before handing in their work to be marked, you would like them to do a preliminary assessment themselves. They should do this using photocopiable page 189. When they hand their work in, they should include their self-assessment sheet.

7. Comparing drafts

Age range
Nine to twelve.

Group size
Groups of six to eight.

What you need
Two drafts of one child's work, photocopied for each pair.

What to do
It is very important that, before this lesson, you ask the child whose work you intend to use whether he minds others in the group reading and discussing his work.

Ask the children to work in pairs. Give each pair a photocopy of the two drafts. Ask them to read both pieces of work, noting the similarities and differences, and decide which they think is the first draft and why. Tell them to list the ways in which the second draft is better than the first.

Now get each pair to report their decisions to the rest of the group and discuss the criteria used by different pairs. Finally, get the author to talk through the two drafts with the group, explaining why he made the changes observed.

8. Questioning the writing process

Age range
Ten to twelve.

Group size
Pairs.

What you need
Paper, writing materials, prompt questions on the board.

What to do
Tell the class that you want to find out *how* they go about writing, the difficulties they experience and how they overcome these. Explain that while children in the class are likely to find a range of things difficult, individuals might be surprised to know how many other children experience the same difficulties.

In pairs, ask the children to interview each other using the prompt questions below. Children must understand that these need not be rigidly adhered to, and they should add their own questions, following through and probing the answers they receive.

• When do you know that a piece of writing is going to be good?
• When and how often do you reread your writing?
• What do you find difficult when you're writing?
• What do you find *most* difficult?
• Why?
• When did you last experience this difficulty?
• How did you overcome it then?
• How do you usually overcome it?

Finally, ask the children to write a report of the interview they have conducted. (Chapter 2 explains how they might do this.) Reports should be read to the interviewee before being displayed in the classroom, and can be discussed in a follow-up lesson with a group of six to eight children working with the teacher.

What do you find difficult about writing?

9. Running monologue

Age range
Seven to twelve.

Group size
Individuals.

What you need
Tape recorder (or teacher present).

What to do
One way of finding out about the writing process – how individuals go about their writing, what strategies they use and how and when they recognise problems – is, quite simply, to ask. Obviously this cannot, and should not, be done too frequently, but it is a technique which gives valuable insights into the way individual children go about their work.

Select a child in the class and explain what you are interested in and why. It is best initially to select a child who is fairly confident, but not seen by the other children as clearly the best or the worst writer in the class. Show her how to use the tape recorder. Tell her to say exactly what she thinks as she writes, starting as soon as she opens a book, reads the title or picks up her pencil. You may need to give an example of what you mean.

10. Writer, know thyself!

Age range
Six to twelve.

Group size
Individuals.

What you need
Writing materials.

What to do
Explain to the class that you are interested in how they go about their writing work on a day-to-day basis. Say that, starting at some time in the near future, you intend to choose one child to observe closely each lesson. No one will know who has been selected, but you will note down your observations of the work pattern and will make a point of discussing your observations with the child afterwards.

Begin by selecting one of the quietest children in the class. Note the following details:
• How does the child settle to work?
• Does he have any particular routines for organising paper, pencils, erasers and so on?
• When does the child stop writing, and why?
• When does the child make contact with other children? Why?
• When does the child move? Why?
• How does the child deal with problems?
• How does he deal with interruptions?

After each observation period, discuss what you have seen with the child concerned. The child should not feel that he is being reprimanded in any way, but the discussion should end with a clear plan of action to help the child work more productively. This should be recorded in the child's words, and a copy kept by both child and teacher.

11. Topic choices

Age range
Six to twelve.

Group size
Individuals.

What you need
One page reserved at the front or back of writing books.

What to do
It is interesting to keep a record of the range of topics that a child writes about in her personal or imaginative writing. Each child should reserve a page at either the front or the back of her writing book or folder and on it list each title or topic she has written about. Periodically, the teacher should assess the range and variety of topics on the list, noting particular interests the child has and the type of topic with which she obviously feels most comfortable or inspired. This information should be used to discuss how and why the child chooses a topic, and to encourage experimentation across a broad range of subject matters.

12. Writing criteria

Age range
Eight to twelve.

Group size
Pairs.

What you need
Large sheets of paper, felt-tipped pens.

What to do
Before the children begin to write a particular story, letter or report, ask them to work in pairs and compile a list of the criteria which could be used to judge the quality of that particular piece of writing. Ask them *how* they will know whether it is a good story, letter or report. Ask them to think about why their criteria are important. This will obviously depend to some extent on the reasons for writing or reading the final script.

After the writing, ask the children to reread their criteria and use them to assess the work done by themselves and by their partners.

Finally, the partners should discuss how their writing could be altered in order to meet the criteria more successfully.

13. The writing conference

Age range
Six to twelve.

Group size
Individuals.

What you need
Writing materials.

What to do
The best way to find out how children feel about their writing, the strategies they use, the problems they experience and the solutions they find, is to ask them. Questions such as 'How did you decide to begin your writing in this way?' or 'How did you decide what to write about?' can tell you a lot about the child's intentions in writing the piece. The sensitive teacher listens for both what the child says and what the child omits to say.

Writing conferences do not have to be long; they may last just a few minutes. The aim of the conference should be to understand the child's hopes for the writing and her perception of the difficulties. A conference should help her identify problems and explore strategies which might offer ways forward, as well as giving support and encouragement. Obviously, one conference would not focus on all these aspects, but it is important to touch on them periodically.

Talking about the writing process helps to improve children's work because it makes them more reflective, more conscious and therefore more in control of what they do. It also gives the teacher invaluable insights into the child's thought processes.

14. Staff development: assessing work

Age range
Adults.

Group size
Any.

What you need
Photocopiable pages 190 and 191.

What to do
Ask each member of staff to 'mark' the work on the photocopiable pages 190 and 191. They should comment on the strengths and weaknesses of each piece, writing their comments on the back. Finally, they should put the list in order of merit; if these children were in their class, which would they consider to be the better and which the poorer?

Ask the teachers to share their comments and overall quality judgements with one other member of staff. Together they should work to compile a list of the features they 'mark', and discuss the relative weighting they give to these.

Finally, ask the pairs to report the main points of their discussion to the rest of the staff.

After the discussion, ask teachers to consider privately how far the comments they write on the bottom of children's work reflect the range of strengths and weaknesses listed at the start of the meeting.

CHAPTER 12

Recommended reading

The following list provides details of a range of useful books about teaching children writing. The books approach the subject in a variety of ways, but they all give sound, practical advice in an interesting and readable form.

We have added a brief description of each book to help you select the ones which will be most suitable for your needs.

Anderson, Lois Napier (1987) *Change: One Step at a Time* (University of Toronto Publications). This book explains how to show children new ways of working and teach them to take responsiblilty for their own work. It gives sane and practical advice for teachers with large classes.

Bissex, Glenda (1981) *Gnys at Wrk: A Child Learns to Write and Read* (Harvard University Press). Bissex describes how her son learned to read and write, and offers interesting insights into invented spelling and reasons for writing.

Calkins, Lucy (1983) *Lessons from a Child* (Heinemann). This focuses on one child and her development as a writer.

Calkins, Lucy (1986) *The Art of Teaching Writing* (Heinemann). Once you begin reading this book, it's hard to stop! Calkins describes how real teachers in real classrooms go about teaching children to write. It is down-to-earth and practical, yet also thought-provoking and inspirational. If you read nothing else, read this.

Gentry, J. Richard (1987) *Spel...Is a Four-Letter Word* (Scholastic Publications). An inspiring book for all bad spellers, reformed and otherwise.

Graves, Donald (1983) *Writing: Teachers and Children at Work* (Heinemann). This practical introduction to the subject describes how to introduce to a class the ideas of selecting topics, drafting, publishing and holding writer workshops.

Johnson, Paul (1990) *A Book of One's Own* (Hodder & Stoughton). This unique book provides a comprehensive guide to book-making.

Michael, Bill (1989) *Purposeful Drawing* (Jordanhill College Publications, Glasgow, Ref. B246). A guide to help teachers develop the young child's communicative powers through drawing.

Michael, Bill and Jackson, W. (1986) *Foundations of Writing* (Scottish Curriculum Development Service). A scheme for teaching writing to infants which focuses on both the composing process and the conventions.

The National Writing Project (1989) *Audiences for Writing, A Question of Writing, Becoming a Writer, Responding to and Assessing Writing, Perceptions of Writing, A Rich Resource: Writing and Language Diversity, Writing and Micros*, (NCC/Nelson). Practical classroom examples underpinned by strong theoretical principles.

SCOLA (1982) *Mr Togs the Tailor: A Context for Writing*. A case history showing how one class creates a character and a context for writing.

SCOLA (1986) *Responding to Children's Writing*; (1982) *Hand In Your Writing*. These books explore how current theories of writing can be applied in practical, interesting ways.

Torbe, Mike (1977) *Teaching Spelling* (Ward Lock). A reader-friendly guide which draws together all the research on children's development in spelling, and is strong on diagnosing spelling errors.

A T CHARTS

England and Wales

The chart on this page refers to the National Curriculum for England and Wales. Use this chart to identify the attainment targets covered by the activities in this book. Activities are identified by their chapter and activity numbers; for example, **1**/5 means Chapter 1, Activity 5. Chapters 3, 5 and 7 are divided into three sections; 'Ourselves', 'Holidays' and 'School' – activities in each of these sections are marked with the letters O, H or S. Therefore, **7**/O/1 means Chapter 7, 'Ourselves' Activity 1. **9**/C/1 means Activity 1 of the 'Conventions in a context' section of Chapter 9.

AT \ Level	**3** Writing	**4** Spelling	**5** Handwriting	**4/5** Presentation
1	**1**/1-5, **2**/1-6, **3**/O/1-7, **4**/1-5, **5**/O/1-3, **6**/1-9, **7**/O/1-7, **8**/1-5	**1**/1-5, **9**/1,2	**1**/1-5, **9**/1,2	
2	**1**/1-5, **2**/5-12, **3**/O/1-7, **3**/H/1-8, **4**/1-9, **5**/O/1-3, **5**/H/1-5, **6**/1-16, **7**/O/1-7, **7**/H/1-8, **8**/1-8	**1**/1-5, **9**/4-6	**1**/1-5, **9**/3	
3	**1**/1-9, **2**/6-14, **3**/H/1-8, **3**/S/1-10, **4**/4-12, **5**/H/1-6, **5**/S/1-8, **6**/10-20, **7**/H/1-8, **7**/S/1-8, **8**/1-16, 19	**1**/1-9, **9**/4-10	**1**/1-9, **9**/3	
4	**1**/1-10, **2**/11-18, **3**/S/1-10, **4**/8-19, **5**/H/1-6, **5**/S/1-8, **6**/12-21, **7**/H/1-8, **7**/S/1-8, **8**/4-19	**1**/1-10, **9**/4-14, **9**/C/1-5	**1**/1-10, **9**/3, **9**/C/1-5	
5	**1**/1-10, **2**/12-18, **3**/S/1-10, **4**/10-19, **5**/S/1-8, **6**/12-21, **7**/S/1-8, **8**/7-19			**1**/1-10, **9**/4-14, **9**/C/1-5

Scotland

The chart on this page refers to the writing component of the Scottish curriculum for English language. Use this chart to identify the strands covered by the activities in this book. Activities are identified by their chapter and activity numbers; for example, **1**/5 means Chapter 1, Activity 5. Chapters 3, 5 and 7 are divided into three sections; 'Ourselves', 'Holidays' and 'School' – activities in each of these sections are marked with the letters O, H or S. Therefore, **7**/O/1 means Chapter 7, 'Ourselves' Activity 1. **9**/C/1 means Activity 1 of the 'Conventions in a context' section of Chapter 9.

Strand / Level	1 Functional writing	2 Personal writing	3 Imaginitive writing	4 Punctuation and structure	5 Handwriting and presentation	6 Spelling	7 Knowledge about language
A	**1**/1-5, **2**/1-6, **3**/O/1-7	**1**/1-5, **6**/1-9, **7**/O/1-7, **8**/1-5	**1**/1-5, **4**/1-5, **5**/O/1-3	**1**/1-5	**1**/1-5, **9**/1	**1**/1-5	
B	**1**/1-5, **2**/5-12, **3**/O/1-7, **3**/H/1-8	**1**/1-5, **6**/1-16, **7**/O/1-7, **7**/H/1-8, **8**/1-8	**1**/1-5, **4**/1-9, **5**/O/1-3, **5**/H/1-6	**1**/1-5, **9**/5, 6	**1**/1-5, **9**/3	**1**/1-5, **9**/4	**1**/1-5, **9**/5-7
C	**1**/1-9, **2**/6-14, **3**/H/1-6, **3**/S/1-10	**1**/1-9, **6**/10-20, **7**/H/1-8, **7**/S/1-8, **8**/1-16, 19	**1**/1-9, **4**/4, 6-12, **5**/H/1-6, **5**/S/1-8	**1**/1-9, **9**/5-7	**1**/1-9, **9**/3	**1**/1-9, **9**/4, 6, 8-10	**1**/1-9, **9**/5-7
D	**1**/1-10, **2**/11-18, **3**/S/1-10	**1**/1-10, **6**/12-21, **7**/H/1-8, **7**/S/1-8, **8**/4-19	**1**/1-10, **4**/8-19, **5**/H/1-6, **5**/S/1-8	**1**/1-10, **9**/5-7, 11, 13, 14, 17	**1**/1-10, **9**/3, **9**/C/1-5	**1**/1-10, **9**/4, 6, 8-10, 12	**1**/1-10, **9**/5-7, 11, 13, 14, **9**/C/1-5
E	**1**/1-10, **2**/12-18, **3**/S/1-10	**1**/1-10, **6**/12-21, **7**/S/1-8, **8**/7-19	**1**/1-10, **4**/10-19, **5**/S/1-8	**1**/1-10, **9**/5-7, 11, 13, 14, 17	**1**/1-10, **9**/3, **9**/C/1-5	**1**/1-10, **9**/4, 6, 8, 10, 12	**1**/1-10, **9**/5-7, 11, 13, 14, **9**/C/1-5

PHOTOCOPIABLES

The pages in this section can be photocopied and adapted to suit your own needs and those of your class; they do not need to be declared in respect of any photocopying licence. Each photocopiable page relates to a specific activity in the main body of the book and the appropriate activity and page references are given above each photocopiable sheet.

Introductory activity: more collaborative decisions, page 17

WISHES

Wish 1

Wish 2

Wish 3

RULES OF THIS SCHOOL

3.

4.

HOLIDAY FRIENDS

3.

4.

Clothes for all seasons, page 38

What do you wear?

sun

rain

snow

wind

Hidden treasure, page 30

North west turret — Store room — Entrance hall — North east turret

Portcullis

Great door

Great hall

Bed chamber 1
Bed chamber 2
Bed chamber 3
Grand bed chamber
Bed chamber 4
Bed chamber 5
Bed chamber 6
Bed chamber 7
Bed chamber 8

Dungeon

Lesser hall

Ball room

Servants' quarters

Moat of despair

Kitchen

South west turret

Banqueting hall

South ea

Back door — Boats

Father Christmas at home, page 59

Father Christmas's favourite meal

Father Christmas's favourite TV programme

The funniest thing that ever happened to Father Christmas

What Father Christmas wears at home

Father Christmas when he was a little boy

I saw it happen. The car was going very fast.

Have you been drinking?

I just didn't see him coming.

The car didn't stop at the red light.

Fred Clarke, 45 years old, plumber.

Delicious treats on sale today!

1. _____

2. _____

3. _____

4. _____

5. _____

6. _____

Manager:

SURVIVAL KIT

Map	Binoculars
Money	Mirror
Compass	Toothbrush
Gun	Passport
Knife	Rope
Blankets	Pen and paper
Clean socks	Handcuffs
Watch	Chewing gum
Matches	Torch
Food and provisions	Tent
Gift for friendly inhabitants	Spade

WISHES

Wish 1   Wish 2   Wish 3

RULES OF THIS SCHOOL

1._____   3._____
  _____   _____

2._____   4._____
  _____   _____

HOLIDAY FRIENDS

1._____   3._____

2._____   4._____

Teddy bears' picnic

(Picture of invited toy)

Fold

_____ (child's name)

invites

_____ (toy's name)

to a happy picnic

Writing addresses, page 29

Put in: 1. The missing address
              2. The missing greeting
              3. The farewell

Thank you for sending the spell so quickly. These children who have moved in next door are driving me batty with the noise they make, but a little magic should do the trick! I'll let you know how the spell works when we meet at Hallowe'en.

- -

I'm hoping that you will pass by soon. My eight legs are exhausted with running around preparing for your visit. I look forward to ~~eating~~, I mean, seeing you.

- -

I've been feeling sad since we parted last week after the banquet. You looked lovely in that golden gown. I hope we'll meet at the ball on Christmas Eve. I'm having a new crown made for the occasion. Save a dance for me.

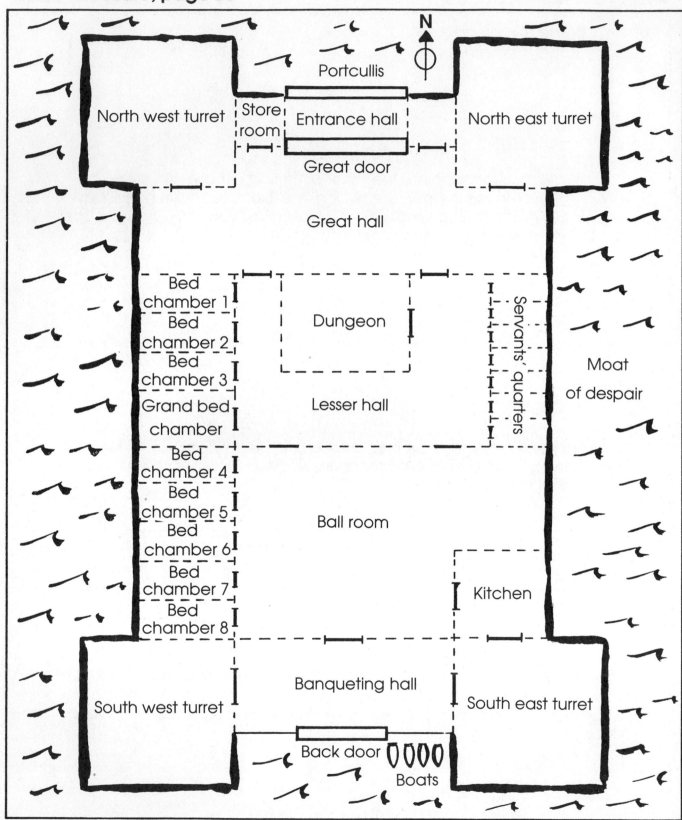

North west turret

Store room

Portcullis

Entrance hall

Great door

N

North east turret

Great hall

Bed chamber 1

Bed chamber 2

Bed chamber 3

Grand bed chamber

Dungeon

Lesser hall

Servants' quarters

Moat of despair

Bed chamber 4

Bed chamber 5

Bed chamber 6

Bed chamber 7

Bed chamber 8

Ball room

Kitchen

South west turret

Banqueting hall

South east turret

Back door

Boats

Fold

Who am I ?

My eyes are

My hair is

My hands are

boy   girl

I am a

Lift this flap to find my picture and my name ↓

What do you wear?

 sun

 rain

 snow

 wind

1. One night I had a dream

2. I saw a strange animal.
   The animal's name was

3. It did a suprising thing

4. I said

5. Then we

Photocopiable pages

Father Christmas's favourite meal

Father Christmas's favourite T V programme

What Father Christmas wears at home

The funniest thing that ever happened to Father Christmas

Father Christmas when he was a little boy

The key, page 61

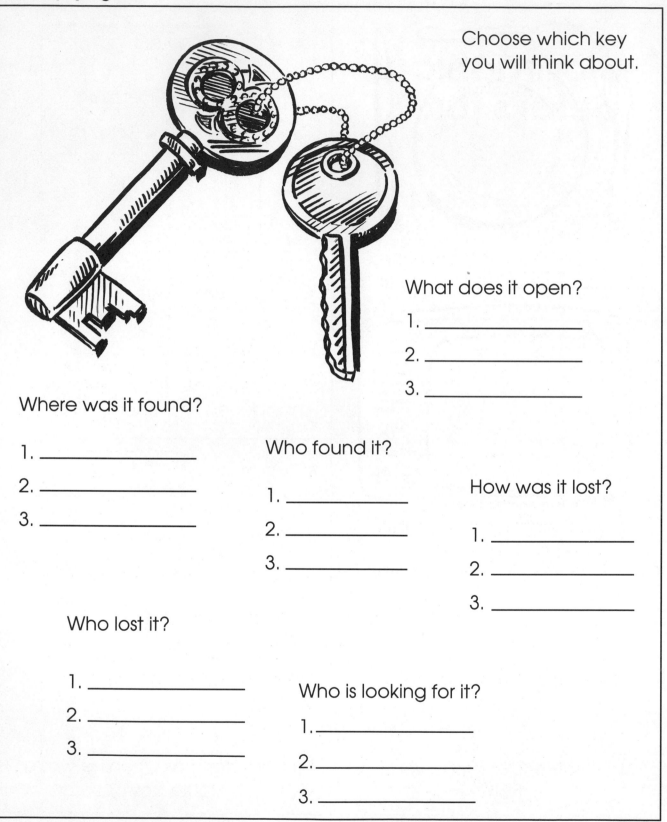

Choose which key you will think about.

What does it open?

1. _____
2. _____
3. _____

Where was it found?

1. _____
2. _____
3. _____

Who found it?

1. _____
2. _____
3. _____

How was it lost?

1. _____
2. _____
3. _____

Who lost it?

1. _____
2. _____
3. _____

Who is looking for it?

1. _____
2. _____
3. _____

Biographical details for:

(stick picture here)

Name: _____

Age: _____   Title(s): _____

Current occupation: _____

Previous occupation: _____

_____

Hobbies: _____

_____

Family _____

_____

Main friends	Name	How long known	Where met
	_____	_____	_____
	_____	_____	_____

Favourite   Food _____   Music _____

T V programme _____

Person most admired _____

The best/worst thing that ever happened was...

I am pleased/angry whenever...

Uncharted island

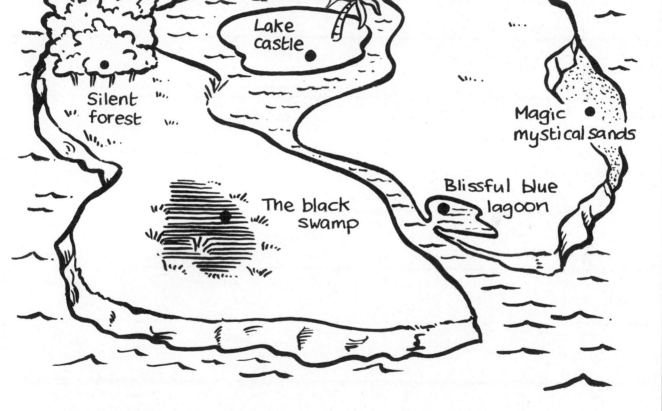

Chapter 1

Shocked and silent, we stared around us. Far away in the distance mountains climbed steeply to the sky, losing their heads in silver clouds. Before us we saw ...

Tastes I like

Tick the box

Name: _____

Food	I like this	I do not like this
apple		
lemon		
onion		
banana		
Choose and draw your own food		

School uniform

Uniform helps all people to look the same, whether rich or poor.	Uniforms look smart.
People should have the right to choose what to wear.	Uniforms help create a school identity.
Uniforms are uncomfortable to wear and inconvenient.	You don't have hard choices to make every morning if you wear uniform.
Uniforms are expensive and old-fashioned.	Clothes are an expression of individuality; why must we all be the same?
Uniforms encourage children to take a pride in their school.	Parents like uniforms; they think they're cheaper.
If you do something wrong and you're in a uniform, people can come and find you.	Uniforms stop you arguing about what to wear for school.

When is handwriting most important?

Writing a note to arrange a meeting with your friend

Writing to your mum when you're on holiday

Writing a shopping list

Writing a letter to complain about something

Taking a phone message for another person

Writing a poem for display on parents' evening

Filling out a job application

Making a poster to advertise the school show

Writing your own secret diary

Writing a spelling test

Questions

1. Why do you think we need to learn how to write?

2. List all the people, both in and out of school, who have read your writing in the past term.

3. List all the different types of writing you have done in the past term, both in and out of school.

4. Who do you write to and what do you write about?

5. What do you think is important about writing?

When is correct spelling important?

Times when it is important

- -

Times when it is not important

It is a shame that Doctor Gill is so poor at punctuation. Can you make sense of her instructions by adding punctuation marks?

One day when I was feeling ill

I paid a call on Doctor Gill

Now that good doctor looked and said

Wear warmer socks upon your head

Put a woolly hat on your knees

Do more praying when you eat your peas

Chew thoroughly when you wash your hair

Use plenty of shampoo when you climb the stairs

At night don't run when you have your tea

Take three spoons of sugar to help you see

Where you've gone wrong

Stop and think

(Never, ever resort to drink)

If all these rules you understand

I guarantee you'll soon feel grand

And rarely if ever you'll need a pill

From Doctor Gill

Spelling is easy. I don't know what the fuss is about.

I'd like to be better at spelling.

All clever children know how to spell.

Spelling doesn't matter to anyone except the teacher.

It's more important to be a good speller than to be a good story-teller with exciting ideas.

Some people can spell, others can't. It's just the way you're born.

If you can't spell you'll never get a decent job.

Spelling is a serious business.

Good readers are good spellers.

All teachers are good spellers.

Most adults are good at spelling.

Good spellers know a lot of spelling rules.

Spelling tests show teachers who the good spellers are.

It's a teacher's job to make sure that children can spell.

Record of work

Topics I have written about this year include:

Title	Difficulty rating (0-5)	Satisfaction rating (0-5)

Signed _____

Name _____

Certificate

This is to certify that _____

uses the following conventions of writing correctly, without needing to be reminded.

M.Y.O. checklist
(Mark your own)

Writer_____ Date_____

Title _____

I have read this work before handing it in.

Signed _____

It makes sense ☐

I've checked the spelling ☐

I've checked the punctuation ☐ sentences
☐ capital letters
I've thought about the
use of language ☐ ☐ speech marks
☐ question marks

Teacher's comments:

Strengths:

Needs:

A Frosty December Morning
by Kirsten Baird

The morning was a frosty one
Even though the lovely red sun was out
The sky looked like the sea with lots
of white waves but now it is changing
to grey
The sun is peeping through the trees
Roof tops are covered in sleet and
so is the ground.
If you look at the windows you can
see the reflection of the sun dazzling
behind the trees
Hungry birds hunting for scraps of
bread because the ground is hard.
Grey clouds coming down over the hill.
The trees have a spooky look about
them.
The roads have ice all along them
The air is fresh today indeed and thats
because it is A frosty December morning.

Coming to School on December morning

The month of december is very cold
It is slippy and icy outside children
are falling all the time Cars are crashing
on the ice. The trees are bare and the
bright sun is shining through them.
Parents doing their shopping are slipping
and sliding. Everyone has coats Scarfs.
gloves. boots and hats on because it
is so nippy. Babies have runny Rosies
The rooves are white with mist. The
clouds are as white as a blankets

A COLD WINTERS MORNING

The golden orange sky
Our breath coming out. soft
Our fingers so cold and numb
The sun shining through the bare
trees
The horses lying in their stables
in soft straw.
Puddles frozen by Jack frost
Childrens cheeks red as rosey's.